MW00356985

Queen Arise!

40 Days to Liberating the Queen Within You

Karin Haysbert

Copyright © 2016 by Karin Haysbert

A Queens For Christ Production

ISBN: 978-0-9976997-0-8

All rights reserved. No part of this book may be reproduced
or transmitted in any form or by any means, electronic or
mechanical, including photocopying, recording, or by any
information storage and retrieval system, without permission
in writing from the copyright owner.

Printed in the United States of America

To order additional copies of this book, contact:

Karin Haysbert, Queens For Christ
support@queensforchrist.org

To the Queens that God has entrusted to me, Olivia and Octavia, and to Queens everywhere who may or may not know that they are Queens yet. To those brave, beautiful souls who have lost sight of their true essence and are in the process of finding it. Arise!

Praises for "Queen Arise" and The Queen

"'Queen Arise' implores every woman to excavate her soul and spirit to find the royal treasure that is often hidden by the opinions of others or veiled behind past traumas. Karin Haysbert takes a brilliant reflective look at her personal experiences and allures her readers to take an intense, introspective examination of their own lives. 'Queen Arise' is a powerful elixir of spiritual and practical wisdom that will detox you of wrong thinking and free the Queen inside of you. The enormously relatable straightforward and applicable 40-day journey gives readers insightful strategies to be Queen!"

Pastor Riva Tims
Majestic Life Church
Orlando, Florida
Author, "When It All Falls Apart"

"I am honored to be able to wholeheartedly recommend my sister, Karin Haysbert's book, 'Queen Arise.' Who is better to teach you than someone who's been through tests and overcome them? Karin is your personal mentor for your spirit and soul work as she details her own transparent journey to you. She breaks the glass ceiling of religion and provokes you to take an inventory of your life so you can move forward and reach your highest potential. If you're ready for freedom and success in your walk with God, your relationships, and your career, then look no further. 'Queen Arise' is the key to unlocking the life you deserve!"

Liris Crosse
Supermodel, Actress, Motivational Speaker
Life of a Working Model Bootcamp
"'Queen Arise' is a masterpiece and a must-read for every woman

who feels the Queen inside is ready to rise to her throne! Karin Haysbert has crafted a book that is bold and in your face yet soothing and comforting with truth. She shares candid stories from her own journey that will make you laugh and reflect. She also poses questions that will stretch you forward into manifestation of your higher self. I had several conversations with the Queen inside while reading, and I am sure your inner Queen will speak to you while reading, too. It is time for us to arise Queens!"

Tiffany Bethea
Author, Speaker, Coach
Founder of KingdomBOSS

"If you're looking for a step-by-step approach to personal development on a soul level, you will find it in this book! In a very practical way, Karin leads you on a journey to dig deeply within yourself to find the treasure that's been hidden for so long. Karin's wisdom and experience are interwoven in such a way that you just know she's talking directly to you. This book is like a companion guide to a successful life for every woman—no matter what role you fill."

Lori Bell
Author, Creator of "The Yes Process"

"'Queen Arise' is exactly what my soul needed. I've been on a journey this year to fall in love with my authentic self, and this 40-day journey offers a loving 'kick in the butt' self truth. This truth has allowed me to shed some unconscious weight of past hurts, un-forgiveness and complacency that have kept me pinned to my 'play it safe' wall. I am redefining love and myself in a whole new unapologetic way. "

Kristin M. Young
Author, Speaker, Coach
Founder of Living the Vows

"In 'Queen Arise,' Karin uses her life story to offer a compelling look into the frustrations and barriers that often prevent Queens from achieving their full potential of their dreams. This book challenges the reader to seek her sense of truth within. She shares her journey of personal triumph and how she made it through a process of truth and transformation in order to start living the life of her dreams. Karin is very generous with this book. Experience her gift."

Tracey Lanier Thompson
Life Coach
Founder of Visions Coaching

"Karin Haysbert has been gifted with the ability to help you to re-evaluate your life and to propel you forward into the purpose that you have been created for. She helped to light a fire under me to move forward and initiate my dream."

Shanon Cook
Speaker, Mentor, Minister
Gems in Christ

"Karin Haysbert is an anointed woman of faith, full of the Spirit, and skillful in the use of the Word of God. She utilizes practical insights and godly wisdom to empower and bring healing to the women that she serves. Lives are changed with each encounter, and you can visibly see them moving into a position of authority."

Adrienne J. Hollimon
Coach, Motivational Speaker, Minister
Discovering Treasures Life Coaches

Table of Contents

Acknowledgments

Peace Queen!

At the risk of sounding "cliché-ish"... "I'd like to thank God!" Thank you God for this amazing process of becoming the Queen that you made me to be ... a Queen for Christ! I am thankful for this blessed journey of becoming!

Thank you to my amazing husband, Brian Haysbert. Your abiding love and devotion is such a comfort and strength to me. Thank you for living out compassion and acceptance towards me and before me.

Thank you to my wonderful children, Malcolm Bulls, Olivia and Octavia Haysbert. Many times, as a mom, I have felt like I was here to teach you, yet you have been my greatest teachers, at crucial times in my life. Thank you for your love, trust, and forgiveness.

To my mom and dad, St. George and Delois Crosse, thank you!! Not everyone has parents who love them AND live a godly example before them. I do! Thank you! I've grown to love and appreciate you so much more in this journey. Parenting is something else, and you did and do it so well.

Many thanks to my Queen Sista, the bold and the beautiful, Liris Crosse. What can I say? You have always believed in me and encouraged me to go for it. Thank you. You may be the little sister, but I look up to you in so many ways. You are a living example of leaps of faith. I love you.

Thank you, thank you, thank you to Molesey Crawford. You helped to pull this book out of me. Thank you for supporting me in being true to the Queen within and confident in my Truth. I love you and am so very grateful to you.

Thank you to my dear Queen sister friends/family for your incomparable love, prayers, inspiration, encouragement, and support in this journey and always. Thank you! Thank you!! Thank you!!! Kimberly Bolar, Carla Williams, Shanon Cook, Pastor Riva Tims, Constance Parker, Leslie Crosse, Shelley Crosse, Tiffany Bethea, Nicole Davis, Lori Bell, Janet Morris … I love you to Life!

Preface

ARISE:

To awaken; to take form or shape;
to stand up; to get up; to become.

Peace Queen!

Yes! It is time for the Queen within to arise! I am so glad that you are joining me on this journey. Thank you! So why must the Queen arise? Because of the dreams. Do you have a dream? I HAVE A DREAM, actually many! Yes, and so do YOU. But are you free to live them?

Today, I am living the life of my dreams. I'm doing exactly what I knew I wanted to do over twenty years ago—that is to encourage, inspire, empower, and liberate women.

But, I haven't always been here. Over the years, I may have been like you, so caught up in caring for everyone else and their dreams and visions that I had forgotten my own.

I put my dreams on the back burner of life and cut the fire off.

I was a wife, mother, daughter, sister, teacher, friend, speaker, minister, and praise and worship leader...the list went on and on.

I was pulled in so many directions, but few directions were actually moving me into the fullness of what I was called to do. It's easy to fall into the rut of day-to-day life and finally look up one day and wonder...

"Where has my life gone?!"

That's what happened to me. When I reached my late 30s to early 40s, an alarm went off! I realized that I was not living up to my full potential. I felt bound, trapped. I did not feel FREE! I was not working towards my dreams, and in fact, I really had stopped dreaming altogether.

I was tired, frustrated, and even battled with mild bouts of depression. But one day through a series of events, I saw it.

My dreams matter, and it's time for me to live them!

This began my Queen Dream Journey! Further along, I realized that I needed to work on myself in a much deeper way in order to bring my dreams to pass.

If you don't grow, your dream won't go!

My own personal, spiritual, and professional growth journey is why I am here. I had to break free from the religious, cultural, and even self-oppression that I had allowed to hold me captive. Honestly, it is because I got mentors and coaches to help guide me along my path. Trust me, Queen! If you are not working with someone who has already been where you want to go, you are working too hard! When I got a mentor to show me the way, my life began to unfold. Every Ruth NEEDS a Naomi. God designed us to need one another.

We thrive in community, but we rise in mentorship!

With that in mind, I created this book and 40-day discourse to document what came out of me in my own Queen Dream Journey.

Why 40? In the Scriptures, 40 is a number of testing and trials, but it is also a number of great truth, transition, and transformation.

We are in our mother's womb for about 40 weeks from conception to birth. We spend 40 weeks within and then we leave that world to enter into a new world.

In the days of Noah, it rained on the earth for 40 days and 40 nights. God was cleansing the earth of an old age, freeing it from its wickedness to create a new one.

The children of Israel spent 40 years in the wilderness being tested, tried, and purged before they entered the promised land of Canaan, the land that flowed with milk and honey.

After Jesus was crucified and resurrected, he appeared to his disciples on the earth for 40 days, assuring them that he was indeed alive, before he then ascended.

It is my prayer that the 40-day pilgrimage you take in this book will begin your process of truth and transformation. I hope that as you go within, take an honest look at yourself and your life without judgment, and tune into what the Spirit is saying to you, you will begin to see yourself in a whole new way. May you ascend! Allow your Queen to arise. May your soul be purged and cleansed, and may you enter into your promised land!

My dear Queen Sister, I wrote this to empower you and, in a way, to mentor world shakers like you to take the leap into your zone of greatness, to free the Queen in YOU. Queen Arise is for you if you:

- know that there is greatness within you and you're ready to bring it to the forefront;

- realize that there are areas of spiritual and personal development that you must attend to so that you can position yourself to walk in your purpose;

- are teachable and willing to humble yourself so that you can learn and grow;

- accept that your "comfort zone" is anything but comfortable and you are ready to be challenged, go beyond your comfort zone, and move into your destiny;

- are willing to go within and to look at what's really going on so that you can make adjustments; or

- are REAL and want real talk!

Queen, if you are looking for a religious discourse or theological discussion, WRONG book. I do offer scriptures in it. However, I'm growing and dying daily to the bondage of religion and coming alive to life in a deeper relationship with God based on all Truth. You will find a Queen's journey to the

Truth of WHO I AM. And honestly, Queen, I am sharing some very personal parts of me in this book about love, forgiveness, self-forgiveness, overcoming childhood pain, letting go, creating peace, sex, and so on.... Need I say more? I am making myself quite vulnerable many times. Read my stories, my grappling, my trials, and my triumphs and find yourself in them. Let God speak to you. Talk to Him. Pour out your heart before Him. I know that they will help you to go deeper. See yourself in a new way. I'm with you. GOD is always with you. Liberate the Queen within! Queen arise! She's been waiting to be freed. I know that you sense her call. Here's something to consider in your discovery...

DIS-COVER
It can be defined as to see, to find, to gain insight.

DIS- to pull apart
COVER- what conceals or hides from view

There is a destiny in us that has become, in many cases, hidden, cloaked, and shielded from view. It's shrouded in fear and buried under beliefs. It is concealed by cultural viewpoints of what we can be, should do, or are worthy of having. It takes Christ in us to excavate the exceptional nature of our entities called "Me" to break through to the brilliance of our being.

And so we DIG!

We dig to unearth the treasure within that is covered with the dirt of all of the lies and limitations that we have accepted as true. We uproot the fibs from others that we have allowed to forge into our reality.

As an emerging shoot, we push through the clods of earth, with our roots digging deeply into the soil of the heart of God within us. We stretch our seedling soul and find our way to the Son, whose rays of Light nourish us from within and we grow outward...

DEEPER AND HIGHER!

My Sister, it's time to let the Queen arise! Let the journey begin!!! With all of the LOVE in my heart!!

**"Trust in Him at all times, you people;
Pour out your heart before Him;
God is a refuge for us. Selah"
Psalm 62:8**

"Arise, shine Queen; for your light has come, and the glory of the LORD has risen upon you."

Isaiah 60:1

Queen, "you shall know the truth, and the truth shall make you free."

John 8:32

"Where there is no vision or dream, the [Queens] perish..."

Proverbs 29:18

"The woman who receives the Dream is not the woman who fulfills it. We all GROW into the Dreams that God places within us."

Karin Haysbert

DAY ONE

Beyond the Zone of Comfort

Peace Queen!

There is a place that feels familiar. It's the place you've always known. It's a place where old landmarks stand firm. Maybe Mama or Grandma lives there. Perhaps, generations of women in your family, your community, or your world camped out there too. Perhaps it wasn't always a really nice place. It may have been cold, rainy, and windy, but for generations, these women made do. They made bricks without straw like the Hebrew slaves. They made something out of nothing.

No, this was not a place of comfort, but because they knew no other way, they made it "comfortable." They did the best they could with what they had. And, when you came along, they gave you the lay of the land. They told you and showed you what to do, what to say, how to say it, and to whom. They told you what was appropriate and inappropriate. They gave you your boundaries. "Don't you dare go out there, but if you do, you must have permission. Until then, wait here within this Zone of Comfort."

But one day, your mind began to open up.

You started to see, really see, the faces of the women in the Zone. You began to hear their hearts, the cries of their hearts with dreams dormant or unfulfilled. You noticed the great gifts and untapped potential lying to waste because they were behind these invisible fences waiting for someone to say, "Come out."

Then, you looked farther and saw other women, strong women too, beyond the barriers. They looked just like the women in the Zone. They were not more intelligent or more anointed. They were not more lovable or worthy. Those women, however, were happy, fulfilled, and free. They stood tall. They spoke their truths. They lived their lives unapologetically.

They were given permission, but by themselves.

They realized that the only limitations were those they put on themselves, so they decided one day to free themselves. They went to the edge that looked so threatening and stepped beyond the Zone. They inched by, with hearts pounding and palms sweating, and a shift occurred, a chain fell, a limitation was lifted, and they just kept going. The more that they walked away, the lighter they felt—the freer they became.

As you watched, you suddenly realized that the women's weary souls within the Zone whose eyes you peered into with great sadness were your own. Yes, your mom might be there. Your sister may be, too. Your pastor's wife and even the lady next door, but until you step beyond the line drawn in the sand of your own soul, beyond the Zone of Comfort and into the Unknown where Truth is known, you're really looking at YOU.

So today, just take one step.

Be open. Be willing to go. The Zone certainly hasn't served you, or at least it no longer is serving you, and honestly it may be familiar, but it is far from comfortable. Your freedom and victory is waiting for you, beyond the Zone of Comfort and into the Zone of PEACE and PROSPERITY. Step out!"

Queen Reflections...

What is something or someone who you've allowed to keep you stuck in the "Zone of Comfort"? How have you been affected? What's one thing that you will do NOW to cross that invisible yet powerful line drawn in the sand of your soul? Write about it!

For more on this chapter, go to www.queenarise.com.

_____

_____

_____

_____

_____

_____

_____

_____

_____

_____

_____

_____

DAY TWO

Love Never Fails

Peace Queen!

Love.
It's not something that I do.
It is something that I am.
I am love.

Love is the essential makeup of WHO I am. It is how I naturally, normally respond. It is what I most easily and freely give when I'm not resisting.

Love is what I most instinctively want to receive. It is what I desire most in my life and for the lives of others.

Love is my greatest friend. Love is my most thorough teacher. Love is the lens through which I can CLEARLY see life's lessons.

Love is my greatest test and yet love is the answer to every question on the test.

Love is my compass, my gyroscope, the GPS of my soul. Without love, I'm lost, going to and fro, trying to find my way in a dark place that light eludes. Love lights the candle, the candle of my soul. It allows me to really see what's happening.

Love allows understanding, compassion, and patience. Love empowers me to take a deep breath, to hold another's hand, or even to hold my own hand, and to say with assurance that "it will be all right" and believe it.

Love raises my awareness. It gives me a heart for the hurting. Love can be tough, but it is usually very tender. Love gives acceptance even when I'm out of line. Love gives hope when all seems lost. Love shows me that brighter days are coming.

Love talks to me and tells me how marvelous I am. Love whispers "sweet somethings" into the ear of my spirit and awakens the sleeping parts of me.

Love re-energizes me, recharges me, and renews me. Love is like the tall glass of ice-cold water on a hot sunny day. It quenches the thirst of my inner being, calms the rumblings of my hungering soul's belly, and it fills me up.

Love satisfies. Yes, love is the greatest thing, and indeed...

Love Never Fails!!

Queen Reflections...

How do you see love in your life? What does it represent to you? Is it your reason for being? Write about what comes up for you.

Karin Haysbert

DAY THREE

Shift!

Peace Queen!

Today my world was rocked. I've been challenged to my core. Everything I've believed is being put on the line. Well, not everything, but enough to make me shake within. I know how my beliefs are being challenged or rather asked, bidden to come higher. I know the terror of being alone, feeling lonely. I think I've already experienced enough of that to not be afraid but… I am.

Rejection seems to be the reflection of my unveiled soul.

Yet, I know my ultimate acceptance of the Truth of WHO I am is asking me to join her at the front. Not from the nosebleed section or even the B or A section but front row, at the 50-yard line in the middle of it all. Usually those seats bring squeals of delight. "I'll be right there in the thick of things," but now those coveted seats almost seem like punishment. Why me? Why couldn't I just be "normal"? So many people are and seem successful in doing so. Why do I have to be "off of the grid," seemingly "off in left field," hung out to dry?

The Truth is that "hanging in" has caused me to dry. So dry that my inner being craves the cooling of tears, the release of which lets out the frustration, the boredom, and the exasperation of church as usual and commonplace life.

We are divine—divine beings clothed in flesh and given license to rule the earth, made in God's image and likeness, chips off of the old block. Only, the chips have forgotten the substance from which we came. We came to fulfill purpose and destiny that transcends flesh. But instead of reaching to the rivers of living water within us to manifest that, we've been dying of thirst.

Thirst for significance through worldly achievement, denying the Power that achieved it. So many have not recognized that the Creator makes all creation, whether we acknowledge it or not. We are living, breathing images of God and as we tap into and become aware of WHO we all are, all we do can become easy, almost effortless. It's like plugging an appliance into the wall outlet and cutting it on. Only, the outlet is within and it allows us to flow outwardly in the beauty of God's magnificent creation.

Going within makes us blossom without and the things that divide us fall in the presence of God's divine love.

So, today, I affirm...I AM loved...I AM accepted...I AM acceptable...I AM divine...I AM!

Queen Reflections...

How have you been challenged to shift, to come higher? Are you afraid to leave others behind as you ascend? Are you frightened that your circle may change, that they might not "get you"? What comes up for you?

_____

_____

_____

_____

_____

_____

_____

_____

_____

_____

_____

_____

_____

_____

_____

_____

_____

_____

_____

DAY FOUR

She's Waiting!
My Inner Girl Gabbing

Peace Queen!

Today, I woke up with the keen awareness of her. She's waiting…still waiting. Waiting to be acknowledged. Waiting to be heard. Waiting to be paid attention to. Waiting to be noticed. Waiting to finally become my priority, to be important to me.

I cannot change the past. I cannot change that I felt overlooked, unimportant, and as a burden to my own parents. I cannot change that I felt invisible to them. Of course, that is not at all how they felt, but it is how I perceived things in my immaturity. I can, however, change how my inner child feels NOW and help her to help me forgive and release all of the residue of the past pain that seeks to imprison me and keep me feeling small, unworthy, incapable, and shackled to the fear of rejection. I can love this little girl into wholeness.

She—I—was born whole...loud...free...confident... knowing what she wanted and not afraid to ask, cry, and demand it, even fully expecting to receive it. She was full of joy! Full of peace! She—I—explored and was never afraid of failing or falling or of what anyone else thought of her. She was who she was and that was more than enough. I think that's part of why Jesus says that we can only enter the kingdom "as a little child," that is with freedom and almost reckless abandon of knowing who we are and that we ARE worthy with childlike faith and trust.

So today, I talk to little Karin Crosse and say,

"I want you to know just how beautiful you are and how completely...

I...LOVE...YOU!!!

I adore you! You are wonderful. You are artistic. You are gifted. You are intelligent. You are funny. You are insightful. You are wise beyond your years. You are a joy to be around. I want you here, right here with me. You are so important to me. From the top of your head to the soles of your feet, you are perfection! And, you are safe. I've got you! I will protect you and provide for you. You never have to worry about a thing ever again. I'm here for you.

So what do you want to do today? What would make you smile? We can go for a walk, jump rope, or play Jacks. Hopscotch or Hula-Hooping would be fun. How about playing with dolls? Want to color? I have a coloring book. Whatever you want to do, we'll do. We can play with Olivia and Octavia. They love you, too! They love to play with you! Your wish is my command. Let's do it. And, if you just want to lie down and talk and watch the clouds float by or do nothing at all but just BE together, that's OK, too. You are so important to me. I want to hear your voice, what you're thinking, and what's on your mind. I LOVE YOU! I'm sorry that I haven't told you more often. Please forgive me. Thank you for your love. From the depths of my heart to yours,

Queen Karin

Queen Reflections…

Deep within you is a little girl who may be hurt, afraid, or lonely. We all need to heal and nurture our inner child. She needs your love. She needs your acceptance. Get quiet and listen to what she has to say. What does she need from you? Write it down, and then give it to her.

_____
_____
_____
_____
_____
_____
_____
_____
_____
_____

DAY FIVE

Releasing the Reins to Let God Reign in Me!

Peace Queen!

Control

It's something that we as divine beings want so desperately but are often so poor at handling. We want to control life. We tell it every way what it's supposed to be. We want to control every situation, to be in charge, and to make our own way. Now, don't get me wrong, there is great power in acting in your power to change you and creating your destiny. The problem comes when we want to use the same measures of control that are meant to effect change in our souls to force change in someone else's soul.

In relationships, control is deadly. What we fail to realize is that we don't need to control anyone other than ourselves. Truth is, the root of the need to control is really fear!

Be honest, Queen. We're afraid that if we don't map out every step of our lives or our children's lives, we might miss it. We're terrified of what might happen to them if we don't pick all of our kids' friends and hover over them. We are afraid that their lives will fail and also that we will feel like bad mothers.

Can we just be honest? Sometimes, we're scared that if we don't know everything about our significant others or spouses, what they're doing, where they are, all about their past, then something may come up that will sabotage our relationships. We make five-year plans, ten-year plans, twenty-year plans, and if we don't get there, then we become worried that something might be wrong with us.

Control. These may seem extreme, but I promise you that they are not. The carnal mind is clever at hiding the severity of our own dysfunction. Planning and having a vision is crucial. I do it. I have plans. I do; however, I add one thing to my plans and my prayers:

"Or something better."

As much as I have grown and stretched spiritually, mentally, emotionally, and physically, I still know that the plans that God has for me are far beyond all that I can ask, think, or even imagine (Ephesians 3:20-21). The cool thing is that it is according to the power that is in ME. He's placed the power in me to bring it to pass. So while I do write the vision and make it plain, I leave room for God.

Always, leave room for God.

I'm flexible and willing to change. I let go of the reins of control. I let God show me instead of me telling Him. I open

38

my heart and mind to something better. Something way better. Something far larger. I let God REIGN in me! So today, let Him reign!

Queen Reflections...

OK Queen. Be honest. Where have you held on too tightly? Where have you decided to be in charge that you need to release and let God lead you? Real talk! Start writing.

_____

_____

_____

_____

_____

_____

_____

_____

_____

_____

_____

_____

_____

_____

_____

_____

DAY SIX

It's Time for a Spiritual Heart Bypass

"These people honor me with their lips but their HEARTS are far from me."

Mark 7:6

Peace Queen!

So Queen, where is YOUR heart? Where are the depths of your soul leaning towards really? It's so easy to fall into the routine of saying, "Praise the Lord" and "God is good all the time," but do you really praise Him? Do you really feel like God is good all of the time to YOU?

Queen, your life is a reflection of your heart. So check yourself? Look around you. What's really in your heart?

41

If LACK is around you, it's in your heart. If CONFUSION confounds you, it's in your heart. If BLESSINGS overtake you, it's in your heart. If JOY overflows in your life, it's in your heart.

It's time that we as Queendom women take greater responsibility for our lives and in accepting that our hearts' conditions, our souls' atmospheres are the fabric upon which our lives are patterned.

We are the seamstresses. We are the tailors. Stop looking outside of you. Stop pointing the finger at everyone and everything else and look at YOU!

What am I thinking about me? What do I believe is possible for me? What limitations am I putting on myself? What blessings have I stopped because I didn't feel worthy of them? How do I feel undeserving?

The truth will set you free, but the facts can keep you bound for sure. Queen, it's time for a spiritual heart bypass. Here's how to do it:

1. Face it: Face it head on. Don't deny it!

2. Feel it: Stop suppressing it. Be honest with yourself. Feelings buried don't die. Acknowledge them so that you CAN let them go.

3. Release it: Now, let it go. Accept that it's no longer serving you. Lean on God's strength to empower you to love, forgive, and let it GO.

4. Replace it: Fill yourself up with God's Love. Fill

yourself with God's Words about you. Meditate on it. Speak it. LIVE IT!

Start doing your heart surgery. Queen, your spiritual arteries have been clogged. Clogged with fear, doubt, and unbelief long enough. Start removing the blocks, displacing them with the Truth.

Here's the truth that I settled within me.

I AM worthy. I AM deserving. I AM the righteousness of God. I have a right to the blessings of God. I AM increasing in favor with God and with man. I walk in continual blessings. All things work together for my good. I love God with all of my heart, mind, soul, and strength. I love myself. I forgive myself. I accept myself. I love, forgive, and accept others, too. The wisdom of God flows with Him. My life is unfolding as it should.

I AM a Queen! I was made to reign!

Queen Reflections…

So where is your heart? Is it far from God? What's in your heart that you know is blocking your good? What's clogging your current? Write. Release it and get your divine flow moving!

DAY SEVEN

Opening the Drain

Peace Queen!

What is Truth…the Truth for me? Truth is…I love God! I am in love with God. I am so thankful for WHO God is and how He has made me. I believe that there is so much to God, more than I or any one person, religion, institution, or anything that walks within the limitations of these earthen vessels can fully comprehend.

I believe in my roots in religion—God the Father, God the Son, and God the Holy Spirit. I also believe that God is me and in me. I believe that I am divine. I believe that God is God (capital G) and that I am god (small g). Read your Bible. I'm made in God's image and likeness. I am a representation of God in part, not in entirety, formed within flesh, but still strong and powerful and able to be and do based on His mighty power within me. I believe that my only limitations are the ones that I place or allow to be placed upon me looking through the eyes of flesh, worldly thinking versus heavenly thinking. I am here to show how flesh doesn't have to hinder me, that I really am more than a conqueror through Christ. I believe that is part of all of our assignments.

I believe that God is neither male nor female because God is Spirit. However, God demonstrates both male and female, even as we do. I believe that God the Father represents the masculine part of God. Years ago, my pastor at the time taught us that the Holy Spirit represents the feminine part of God. I didn't get it then. I put it on the shelf and now, 20 years later, I SO get it. And perhaps, God the Son came to show the emerging Power of the oneness and balance between both. Perhaps it is how when we only DO, which is the masculine, what we see the Father do, then we can ALLOW, which is the feminine, the Spirit of God to flow through us without measure as Jesus the Christ did. I think about these things.

I'm very acclimated in seeing God as Father, especially in this patriarchal society and culture in which I was raised and now live. However, I'm open and learning to see God as Mother too, as Divine Feminine, the Holy Spirit, more and more and in letting Her lead and guide me into all Truths, as the scriptures say, and as She did with the Son on earth. I believe that Jesus came to show us a new consciousness, a new way of thinking, living, and being. I believe He released or rather helped to unlock a Christ Consciousness in us all called the Mind of Christ. Jesus showed us that we are supernatural beings and can live as such. I see Jesus as fully God and fully man. I believe that He came to show us the way to the kingdom...that the kingdom of God is within us.

The difference is Jesus came to earth REMEMBERING and we mostly came to earth forgetting WHO we are. So we are all going back to the future. The Word says that kingdom is Righteous, Peace, and Joy in the Holy Spirit (Romans 14:17).

When we rightly align ourselves with God's way of BE-ing, we will do the greater works, walking in the peace, joy, and rightly ordered steps that Her divine love provides.

I am gaining clarity. I'm open and my foundation remains strong, even as I build upon it. For me, it's not throwing out the baby with the bath water. It's cleaning the baby, my own consciousness, my thinking about who God is and who I am, from head to toe, and then opening the drain.

Queen Reflections...

So Queen, are you willing to open your mind to receive Truth even if it bucks your religious paradigms? To allow the Queen to arise, Christ in you, you will have to. What comes up for you here? Write about it.

DAY EIGHT

All Fear Is Big

Lessons from a Red Bike, a Couple of Oranges, and a Policeman's Car

Peace Queen!

Today, I continue the quest to love, heal, and reclaim the wonder of my inner child, that part of me that walks in child-like faith that jumps—knowing that Daddy is there to catch me and is assured of Mama's divine love. I see how what I thought was a little thing is actually BIG. Fear. Fear is fear and ALL fear is BIG—whether we think so or not, whether we feel it is or not. ALL fear is separation from God, detachment from our Divine Source, and that's BIG.

About a week ago, out of the blue, or so I thought at the time, I told my husband that maybe I was finally ready to get a bike. I surmised it would be a fun activity to do as a whole family. Bike riding had not really been my thing for many years, but it is something that the girls enjoy doing with Brian.

49

Quite frankly, I felt like it was something that he could do with the girls to give me a break.

So the other day, after we finished our date-night dinner early, Brian started to drive us somewhere other than home. Often, I'll just go with the flow and ride, instead of peppering him with questions. I'm growing into letting it be. We ended up at a bike shop. Oh joy. I wasn't too excited about spending twice as much for a better bike. A Schwinn bike from Wal-Mart would've been fine for me. However, this IS Brian's thing and quality lasts. So, again, I just went with the flow. We picked out a bike and a helmet and bought it. For Brian, that was a big deal. Now, the only problem was that BOTH of the girls needed new bikes because they'd outgrown their current ones. We went to the shop that they usually get their bikes from the next day to pick up their new bikes. They were supremely surprised and equally excited!

Bike riding... Why don't I really enjoy riding, I thought. As the salesman, I'll call him Brad, gave one girl's feedback on how to adjust her turns to avoid tipping her bike over... the fear emerged! Fear is often insidious. It loves to hide in dark places—places that you'd forgotten about or not thought of in a long time—but all the while, fear is steadily dragging you down, holding you back, even if it's just slowing your roll ever so slightly. Fear is there to keep you small, to stop your progress, to stymie your success. As Brad began to recount the numerous times that he had fallen bike riding as a kid, my own memory from yesteryear started to emerge...

I had to be six or maybe seven. I was riding my bike, on the sidewalk outside of our apartment building while trying to hold a couple of oranges. I found my handlebar wobbling as I struggled to steer and to balance my tasty treats. I was losing

50

the battle and instead of letting the fruit go to get control of the bike, I reached for the falling fruit and crashed my bike…into a car…the policeman's car. Then, me, the bike, and the fruit slammed into the pavement. I don't ever remember feeling that much pain, all at once. I felt paralyzed. I'm sure that I cried out because the policeman, a tall, brown man with a perfectly sculpted Afro came running out. He picked up my bike, and me, and took us upstairs to my mom. Funny thing is, I'm not sure what happened to my fruit, which was the thing I tried so desperately to hold onto and was the reason that I crashed in the first place, or so I thought.

Although I don't recall feeling fear about riding my bike or of crashing it right after that, I'm sure that the seed of fear was planted. I don't remember seeing riding ever as a great love, and I did eventually become aware of my fear of being near cars on a bike, but that was years and years later. I rationalized that they might not see me and could hit me. Interesting. Could it simply be the reverse of my not seeing the car and crashing into it? Thinking back to my childhood incident, all I saw was the fruit and my fear of dropping or perhaps losing it. In my mind, I thought, "Oh that's just a little fear." NO.

All fear is BIG. It paralyzes purpose and becomes the obstacle to opportunities.

So, what can I glean from that experience? There are times in life when we need to let GO of something or someone that we want in the moment so that we can grasp or maintain what we really need. I could've easily dropped the fruit in order to get control of my bike and then stopped and gone back to pick them up. So in life, sometimes, we must let GO of a person or a situation to get clear direction for ourselves or to gain our balance. Perhaps, we can revisit them or it later and still enjoy the fruits. Further, if we strive to hold onto fruits, things, people that we must release and do not have balance, harmony, or divine alignment, then we can crash, get hurt, and risk losing it all while experiencing paralyzing pain—that which fear is a master at providing.

How can we shift? When we realize that we live in a plenteous world in which God abundantly supplies all things to us, we don't have to grasp and hold onto things or people beyond their season. We can let the fruit go. We can live in the freedom of detachment, where we can have things but they don't have us. Worry cannot reside in that place. Anxiety is an unwelcome guest. We can let go of our fruits, because we know that there's always MORE! There is ease, grace, flow, and REST. The real fear was the fear of loss, the fear of not having or of God not providing. When we let that go, we can rest.

The scriptures say, "Come to me all of you who are weary and heavy laden and I will give you REST! Take my yoke upon you and learn of me, for I am meek and lowly of heart and you will find REST for your souls." The yoke can also be stated as take my "beam of balance" upon you. When we rest in Him, trust Him, and have faith, it brings balance to us. The reverse is true, too. When we seek balance by getting into alignment with God, His will and His ways, we find rest as well.

I steered clear of bike riding altogether at some point. And my fear that linked bikes and cars grew, unbeknownst to me. What's so compelling is that one of my most profound, tangible experiences with God happened on...you guessed it...a bike, just a few years later. Maybe that's why fear closed the door on bike riding, to keep me from going deeper, to block my brilliance, to intercept the inspiration.

So, today, I'm ready. I'm ready to ride again without fear because I know that I am safe. I'm always surrounded and protected. I am always provided for and abundantly supplied. I'm open. I'm open to how God is going to minister to me, little me, and make me bigger as I let the little fear...the BIG fear....GO!

Queen Reflections...

So how about you, Queen? What's the "little" fear that you have not paid much attention to that could be or has held you in bondage? God has not given you the spirit of fear. (2 Timothy 1:7) Isn't it time to let it go? Write about it.

For more on this chapter, go to www.queenarise.com.

DAY NINE

Happiness Rising!

Peace Queen!

A couple of years ago, the song "Happy" became a force of nature. People from all walks of life, every nation, every culture, and every gender happily danced, clapped, and skipped to the song "Happy." Young and old. Rich and poor. Rough and gentle. All people want to be happy, to clap, to dance, and to feel like their lives have no limits.

But here's the big insight about happiness. You cannot make anyone else happy. That is THEIR responsibility. You may do things that others find pleasing, but their happiness is their DECISION. When I finally got this, I let the weight of the world roll off of my shoulders. I was still trying to do it, in a much smaller fashion and it was no longer consistent with my Truth.

You cannot console the inconsolable.

You can hold space for them. You can pray for them. But it is a black hole that cannot be filled by anyone else but them and God. Stop wearing yourself out trying to do for others what only they can do.

By the same token, no one is responsible for your happiness but YOU. I remember people in the church saying that you should not seek to be happy. Huh? They told me that you should seek to have joy, because happiness was contingent upon what is happening.

Well Queen, I want them BOTH—great things happening for which I can feel great happiness and joy to endure when the great things are on the way. When you decide to be in joy and peace, your happiness will arise. It lifts because what's happening is a lifting IN you, regardless of what's going on around you.

So in this moment, be grateful. Seize JOY. Live in PEACE and let HAPPINESS rise!

Queens Reflections…

Are you happy? No really…are you really happy? If not, why not? Sometimes we think the religious thoughts that tell us that God is not interested in our happiness. Not true. What makes you happy? Write about it. Think on it. Receive it in your life.

DAY TEN

Meditation Is Medication for My Soul

Peace Queen!

Meditation. It's more than a pause, the cessation of activity, or the quieting of my mind chatter.

It's beyond the stilling of the constant motion of my inner being.

Meditation extends past slowing down my breath and calming my oceans' tides within. Meditation is the healing balm. It provides relief—relief from the aches of incessant thought, soothing from the searing patterns that inflame me.

In meditation, I can release what is constantly tapping me on my shoulder, and I can gently show it the door. In meditation,

I bring in new houseguests or awaken others who have been asleep so that they can play together and begin to create and formulate. They, the life-giving, love-affirming thoughts within me, collaborate to show me the way. I strengthen their bonds and it makes me whole within.

In meditation, I set the stage to think a new thought and to strengthen others. I form new beliefs and make others firm. I gained a fresh perspective, another outlook. I am made whole from the inside and in time, not much longer, it spills to the outside when I'm too full to keep it, the vision and imaginations, within.

My meditation becomes MANIFESTATION, because I AM whole. My soul is complete, because of the healing power of meditation.

Thank you! Thank you! Thank you!

Queen Reflections...

So do you meditate? I know people have made it out like it is some weird thing that should be feared. Religion has made it seem as if it's some foreign Eastern thing. Note to everyone... Jesus was born in the EAST! Further, meditation is not scripture memorization. I've seen people who can quote Genesis to Revelation from memory and still live defeated. Meditation is what will change your life and lead you to SUCCESS! See Joshua 1:7-8. It is an inner quieting and picturing that will bring your dreams to life. Write your thoughts about meditation here and go MEDITATE!

DAY ELEVEN

I Am an Author.
Who Are You?

"Before I formed you in the womb I knew you;
Before you were born I sanctified you;
I ordained you a prophet to the nations."
Jeremiah 1:5

Peace Queen!

I am an author! There, I said it! Over a year ago, when I first printed my business cards, I put on it that I was a "writer." Do you want to know why? I was afraid to say that I was an author, because I had not published anything yet. I was afraid to declare what I knew that I was.

Write. Write. And write some more. For the last 20 years, I have written. Now don't get me wrong, I didn't have crystal clarity about the author piece, but I knew I was supposed to write. My husband called me a scribe. When I went to church, I'd take notes. This was something that I didn't see a lot of people doing, but in my mind, it only made sense. How can I review what's been taught without taking notes? We don't go to school without a pen and paper. Why don't we do that at church? But I digress. So I would write and write and write. I didn't write just what the preacher said, but I'd also write what God was saying to ME in between the lines.

Then, I discovered the power of journaling. I would write my thoughts. I'd write my concerns. I'd write my joys. I'd write my sorrows. I'd write when I was happy. I'd write when I was sad.

And then I stopped writing.

I was in such a wilderness. I was in so much pain, that I couldn't even write. The thing that was so natural to me was locked up because of the pain. Gently Mama, the Spirit of God, kept urging me to write, but I was in so much of a fog. I just couldn't see clearly to even grab pen and paper.

About writing… I remember being in school, I don't know if it was in high school or college, but there was a teacher who graded me harshly, and from that point on I felt like I couldn't write. I think I got a C in the class, but I thought I was a better writer but began to believe that perhaps I was not. Here's the key.

I allowed someone else's opinion of me to change my own beliefs about myself.

Are you doing that? So it wasn't until I started to homeschool my children that I realized that I really had a gift. As I taught my girls how to write, I taught myself and built greater confidence in my gift. If I homeschooled only to reveal and release the author in me, it was all worth it! So as I begin to free myself from my fear of expressing my true self and to heal myself from the misguided opinions of others, the author emerged. She was there all of the time.

"Before I formed you in your mother's womb I knew." This is what God told Jeremiah. This is what God is telling you and me. God knew who you were and what He called you to do and the gifts He placed within you to bring about His purposes before time began. So Queen, even though your gift may be in seed form, it's still the gift! Jeremiah was a prophet before he was even sent here. No one needed to tell him that he was a prophet to make him a prophet. He was already one.

Man can only confirm what God has established before time.

Others recognizing your gift is completely different than releasing the gift itself. So here I stood an author, calling myself a writer, because I was afraid that someone would question whether or not I had external validation for the gift.

No, I am INTERNALLY VALIDATED! Validated by God. I know WHO I am. I am an author, among MANY other things. I'm developing the seed into maturity, but the gift is still the gift, and it is marvelous in God's eyes and in mine. Enough said! I stand confidently knowing WHO I am, declaring who I am, and bringing it forward!

I am an author. Who are you?

Queen Reflections...

So WHO are you, Queen? What is your gift to the world? Are you hiding it because it's not fully formed yet? Are you waiting for someone else to validate it and give you permission about it? That ends today! Write! What did GOD say that He knew about you before you came here?

Karin Haysbert

65

DAY TWELVE

A Decision for PEACE

Peace Queen!

Today, I decided to be at PEACE. Yes at PEACE. PEACE does begin with me in my decision to be such. As for me at my house, all which is contained within my physical house, spirit and soul, we will serve the Lord. God is a God of peace. So, I too, am a god of peace.

I woke up this morning with a fresh perspective. ENOUGH! I will not talk about what doesn't bring me PEACE any longer, except in my conversations with God and me. At least that's my objective. God is the one who can help me to change myself, that is to change what is bringing war to my soul, so I'm letting the General, the One who fights my battles, give me the strategies through surrender. Life is not supposed to be constant war. I'm supposed to live in PEACE.

I'm at PEACE. I'm doing what makes me happy and what brings ME the greatest joy. This is not to the exclusion of others, but it is certainly never to the exclusion of myself again. I release everyone else to their highest good and I let them go find it. I let go of my expectations of others. I let my expectations be in God to give me what gives me joy and PEACE whether it includes others or not.

I am no longer afraid. I come from a God of infinite abundance. He has already provided exactly what I need. All that I need to support me and nurture me is at my disposal. I am at PEACE. I know that I have so much to offer and so much to receive. And, now is my time to reap. I will deny myself no longer. I am having all that I desire. I am having fun living. I'm making my time here full of joy. I'm living the life that makes ME happy.

It's my time, my time, right now just because I decided to BE at PEACE! And so it is!

Queen Reflections...

Have you made a decision to be at PEACE? There is power in decision. When you make a clear decision, you CUT OFF all other options. Will you cut off anything that takes you away from your peace? What attitudes, ideas, thoughts, and beliefs do you need to release to live here? Write it and stick to it.

DAY THIRTEEN

Self-Care Is Not Selfish ... It Is the Pursuit of Happiness

Peace Queen!

It's been several years since I began a DEEPER dive into life. Interestingly enough, what created the perfect storm was a deep sense of rejection and lack of appreciation that I felt from a group of women that I co-led in a homeschool co-op. The other significant factor was my aim to embrace myself more, starting with loving and caring for my natural hair. Yes I, like so many, started on the outside...the fruit. However, it took the pressure of pain and the crucible of crisis and change to force me inward.

Let me unpack this. My jump into the natural hair community led me into not just taking care of my hair but examining what I was putting into my body. I was getting closer…. Then, in my quest for natural health, I had several health challenges. I stumbled across the books, "You Can Heal Your Body" and "You Can Heal Your Life." I was already broken open by the pain that I had experienced, and these readings were like salve to my wounded soul. They changed my life!

I started by learning not to blame others for my circumstances, taking responsibility for my life on a deeper level and being more conscious of what I have created. It made me examine my own points of attraction. I've been a soul woman for a long time. The mind has always intrigued and fascinated me. My ministry has consistently been linked to it. These writings simply brought greater clarity.

The Word says that, "the curse causeless shall not come." There's a reason for my madness and, guess what? I'm at the center of it. If I accept that and make changes, I walk in POWER. If I sit around and blame everyone else… " They did me wrong….They didn't appreciate me….The devil is busy…. Well God did you want me to have it….It's my mother's fault….My father is the problem…. My husband is holding me back….If these kids weren't in the way… She stabbed me in the back…" and on and on…

When I blame, I'm stuck and I give away my power. In each situation I face, I am the common denominator and something in me set the stage for that…some thought…some belief.

I came to realize that until I appreciated myself, no one else really would. When I totally value my contribution, and myself, then others will, too. I didn't get it all at once. My first reaction was to separate, withdraw from everything and everybody! Can I tell you what I was really thinking? "Those wenches don't appreciate all my hard work!" I said in my mind of them. Truth was, they were not the problem. I was. I was a "YES" girl. I took on more than I should have, tried and did everything perfectly, because somewhere inside I felt like I wasn't enough.

My perfection played out in such a way so that if anyone rejected me, I could say it was them because I have done everything perfectly. I had dotted every "i" and crossed every "t." I didn't realize the paralysis of this "perfection" until my soul came crashing down and was shattered into pieces. For once, I took an honest hard look at each of those pieces.

So I was broken.

As I put the fragments back together, I stepped out of everything. I went from one extreme in doing everything, in charge, leading to NOTHING. I would do nothing! To the outside, untrained eye, I appeared selfish. I did nothing or little unless it served me. I actually was finally dipping my toe into the stream of self-care. My first answer was, "No." I admit. It was a little empty feeling unattached to activities and leadership. But it was a good feeling of SPACE.

SPACE!!!

Space to think, to consider, even sometimes to brood and fall back into blame a bit...but eventually to take care of myself and to HEAL. Even in my darkest despair, my light was still shining through the cracks. Then here comes the test again, I was being recruited in my new homeschool group for leadership. (I had left the other one where I had my crash and burn.) My answer was "No"! I'm doing nothing! It felt strangely wonderful to say "No," a word that I was not as intimately acquainted with. It felt surprisingly good! I was caring little about what people thought about my "No" and myself. I was doing my own thing. I was taking care of my children and myself. It was liberating to release trying to take care of others at my expense.

Today, as I grapple for balance, I know it's time to go deeper into my own self-care. Yes, I eat healthily, drink water, take supplements, move, meditate, breathe, tap, and get acupuncture and massages, and every now even visit Korean spas. But the self-care that I'm talking about is much deeper. It's greater SOUL care. My focus had been on self-care more on the outside fruits, but I want to focus more on the INSIDE care, the roots, in a more profound way. Taking better care of my mind. Paying closer attention to my own thoughts. Honoring how I feel within my heart. Following my own intuition. Releasing all self-betrayal and people-pleasing. Feeling love and accepting it within myself.

Now that I know that my body speaks what my mind is saying, "I STOP to listen." Now that's self-care that I am always upgrading in. So today, I get a little more self-focused, not to the exclusion of others but for the elevation of me. I put myself back at the TOP of the list in a new dimensional way. My thoughts, feelings, and beliefs are of primary importance to me, and aligning them with God's is my first priority.

Self-care is not selfish. It is the key to life and the pursuit of happiness.

Queen Reflections...

Well Queen, that was a lot! How are you in the caring and keeping of YOU? We run from pillar to post to care for everyone else at times and find ourselves left behind. No more! What can you do TODAY, RIGHT NOW, to take wonderful care of you, inside and out? Start writing and do it!

For more on this chapter, go to www.queenarise.com.

_____

_____

_____

_____

_____

_____

_____

_____

_____

_____

_____

_____

_____

_____

_____

_____

_____

_____

DAY FOURTEEN

Honoring Our Parents In Truth

Peace Queen!

HONOR! It's a word that makes us sit up straighter. It puts a smile on our faces. We hold our heads up and our spirits lift.

> "Honor your father and your mother which is the first commandment with a promise that it may go well with you and that you may live long on the earth."
> **Ephesians 6:2**

Did your spirit just fall? The Ten Commandments gave ten godly guidelines for living. This one was the first with a promise attached: "good, long living." Who doesn't want that? We all want the good life. Then, when life is good, we want more of it!

But what if my blockage to the good life lies in my failure to honor, value, and hold in high esteem the vessels chosen to usher me into this existence? What if my greater joy lies in loving my mom in spite of her imperfections? What if the key that unlocks abundance for me is in acknowledging the greatness in my dad regardless of whether or not he gave me what I thought I needed?

Parents. Frequently, we look at our parents as "perfect." Or, we at least feel like they should be perfect.

We are all perfect beings that express imperfectly based on our perspective.

We all long to get it "right," to do what's "needed," to bring about the "best" in every circumstance even when we do not know how to. We want to even when we are not allowing ourselves to be aware of the path that is laid out before us. We all have hopes and dreams, fears and "failures."

Sometimes we are grown up, but we still look at our parents through the eyes of our hurt, inner child, analyzing everything through her immature reasoning. Here's the Truth that will free you.

Everyone does the best they can with the knowledge, understanding, and awareness that they have at the time.

Your parents included. If we accept this, we can look at our parents maturely. We can give them mercy, the mercy we need daily. We can love them unconditionally with the love that is so freely available and given to us. We can truly forgive them and let them, and most importantly ourselves, off of the hook. The hook has only hurt us and kept us stuck, judging them, blaming them, and magnifying their perceived weaknesses.

Truth is, down on the inside of our moms and dads is a hurting, frightened little girl or boy that seeks love, attention, and approval, just like we do. Don't begrudge them of that. We forget that they are just like us. We place them above us when in Truth they are really beside us. They are beside us on the same journey of discovering their true essence. Their being here longer doesn't make them farther along on their journey.

They are where they are.

Accept that. Learn from them. Love them. Approve of them. Honor them. We must let them know that we care about them, no matter what. We appreciate all that they have done for us.

Truth is, we received exactly what we needed in life for our purpose.

All that we needed for our true soul's unveiling was given to us. Everything fits perfectly into our life's plan and purpose. Instead of cursing the darkness, bless the light. There's so much light there that the momentary glimpses of darkness are swallowed in its brilliance—that is, if we will perceive it, embrace it, and appreciate God's gift to us in our parents.

So today, I take a look at my parents with new eyes. I see them through the eyes of grace and gratitude. I love them, cherish them, and HONOR them... in truth.

Queen Reflections...

Mom and Dad. It's time to take a look at your relationship with them. Do you honor your parents in word and in deed? Do you need to forgive them in order to do so? Can you accept them as they are and simply love and honor them? Write whatever comes up for you on this. It's a key to the abundant life we desire.

_____

_____

_____

_____

_____

_____

_____

_____

_____

_____

_____

_____

_____

_____

_____

_____

_____

_____

_____

DAY FIFTEEN

No Need to Fear... Mama Is Here!

Peace Queen!

Today, I awakened with such a sense of the presence of the Holy Spirit. The words to the song "Holy Spirit" by Jesus Culture flooded my mind. I kept humming and humming it. I didn't know all of the words, but the Life, the substance of them, reverberated within my soul. As I looked in the mirror into my eyes to greet myself with love, my daily ritual, I peered in little Karin's eyes, too. I keep a picture of myself when I was about five years old on my mirror with one of my mirror work cards. It was Christmas at Grandnana and Grandpa's and I'm posing with some of my presents. I sent love to my little one within and noticed the blue and white portable record player, one of my favorite toys, on the table behind me.

That's it! Lil' Karin reminded me of how much I love music and especially singing. She wanted to sit on Mama's lap through this song that rang within me. By now, you know that I consider the Holy Spirit the feminine part of God. So, that's the Mama that I'm talking about.

It had slipped away. I hadn't been singing and worshiping, entering into Her presence regularly in the ways that I normally would have, and my SOUL (through this picture and the words that looped within) were calling me to draw nearer, to become aware of Her presence. She longed to let me know that I am not alone and that She's here. So, I sang. I became aware of Her presence. I experienced Her goodness.

I lifted my voice and raised my hands, entering into worship, and it became infinitely clear. "Oh taste and see that the Lord is good!"

The beauty and essence of the words of that beautiful song began to wash my soul, cleansing me, releasing shame and guilt, annihilating doubt and fear, assuring me of Her loving presence. I'd neglected Her. I hadn't been spending time in Her presence, focused on Her love.

Father's love is different than Mama's love. And what I and Lil' Karin needed was more of the sweetness and ease of Mama's love...more nurture, more care, more tenderness. A hush came over the recesses of my heart as I sensed myself being gently rocked in the arms of the Spirit, on Mama's lap.

She silenced my soul. "Ssshhhh. Be at PEACE my child. I have you in my arms. I am making all things well. No need to fear. Mama is here."

Thank you! Thank you!! Thank you!!!

Queen Reflections...

Queen, there are things that can be accomplished in worship that don't easily happen anywhere else. In God's presence is fullness of joy and at His right Hand are pleasures forevermore. I want you to enter into worship, but before you do, write what you will surrender to God there.

_____

_____

_____

_____

_____

_____

_____

_____

_____

_____

_____

_____

_____

_____

_____

_____

_____

_____

_____

DAY SIXTEEN

The Evaporation of Confusion

"For God is not the author of confusion but of peace..."
1 Corinthians 14:33

Peace Queen!

Confusion is merely a conflict within your soul. Deep within, you already know what to do, but the voices of your past and present often seek to silence your future through fear. Instead of following your heart, going with your gut, your mind introduces all of the "what ifs" and "just in cases." The overload of fear breeds frustration and... confusion.

Silence is in order.

Quiet the voices. Remove all audible sound. Get still and let the Divine voice of love speak. She, the Spirit of God, is always speaking. Mama will tell you exactly what to DO. Get quiet. Get clear on who you are. Go back to the basics.

Do you know who you are? Why are you here? What is the light that you were sent here to shine? What gives you the most JOY? What lightens your step? What lifts you up? What makes your spirit soar? Also, what breaks your heart? What can you almost not bear to see? What puts a holy fervor in you to solve?

In the treasure map of your soul, at the intersection of your greatest joy and your greatest pain, start digging. You will find gold in their hills. In that bounty, is WHO you are and who you are called to uplift. The path unfolds from there.

Truth is…You know what it is. Yes you do! When you clear the clutter of fear's clamoring by getting clear on who you are and what you were sent here to be, the do, the path will become clear.

Confusion exists when fear is on the line.

It's almost like you're on a phone call with your genius, your Highest Self, and a third party joins the call. Fear… fear comes on the line, only when we lose sight of who we are, and one of its fruits is confusion.

Confused Queens wander aimlessly trying to do everything or they do nothing at all. They listen to everything and everybody or don't hear anything.

Clarity of WHO you are brings balance.

It evens the scales, and it allows you to filter words and thoughts with the Truth—the Truth for you. Truth is...what works for one Queen may not be your path. Open to clarity for YOU. Walking it out still takes faith, trust, and bold action, but it is infinitely easier when you feel clear.

Know WHO you are Queens. Rest in who you are. That clarity will cause confusion about what to do to evaporate and allow PEACE to emerge!

Queen Reflections...

What is something that you have felt unclear about? What part of your life screams out for more clarity? Start digging around that area. Who are you in that? What contribution are you here to bring? Get still and allow the Spirit of God to speak to your heart and to reveal more of you to you. Write about it.

_____

_____

_____

_____

_____

_____

_____

_____

_____

_____

_____

DAY SEVENTEEN

Who Makes Your Baby Leap?

Peace Queen!

In Luke, "when Elizabeth heard Mary's greeting, the baby (John) leaped in her womb, and Elizabeth was filled with the Holy Spirit." In a loud voice, she began to prophesy to Mary about the Divine Seed in Mary's womb (Jesus).

Queen, who makes your baby leap? What Queen is in your life that when she comes around you, the divine seed in your womb leaps for JOY? When your Elizabeth comes into your presence, ideas come ALIVE! When you are with her, there is a FLOW in the Spirit as you connect. You NEED a divine midwife. You need a Queen that will help you to nurture and to birth what's growing on the inside of you.

Who is she? Identify her. Cling to her. Pray with her. Connect regularly with her. Bring each other's visions to pass!

Although the gift of God is in you, there is someone outside of you that will help to bring it to pass.

God made us to need each other. It is a part of how He keeps us humble and connected. Trust me, God would not give you a vision that does not need Him and others to fulfill. Acknowledging that and attending to that need in a progressive way is a sign of a maturing Queen. No Queen is an island and no Queen can prosper as such.

Find your Elizabeths! ~Queen arise!

Queen Reflections...

So who is she? You may have several. How do you know that she is the one? Right now, set a concrete plan for how you will connect on a consistent basis. Queen, we do what we want to do—what is important to us. Do it!

_____
_____
_____
_____
_____
_____
_____
_____
_____

Queen Arise: 40 Days to Liberating the Queen Within You

DAY EIGHTEEN

Birthing Your Dreams

Peace Queen!

So it's Christmas Eve. It's the day before we celebrate the birth of Jesus. No doubt, this was a very uncomfortable time for Mary. She was "great with child," as in "Get the Baby Outta Me" mode. They were traveling on long, dusty roads, and she was on the back of a beast. It was not the most convenient place for a laboring mother to be in who is preparing to give birth.

So too, with us, many times, the most glorious "birthings" are inconvenient, uncomfortable, and even downright PAINFUL. We ride the beast, the ego, and it hurts. There's pain, contractions, because what's in us must come OUT. The Queen with the dream must give birth. We go from place to place, and there's nowhere to lay our heads. We feel tired, restless, ready to give up, but then we find a place, an unlikely place, but the perfect place to stop, rest, and to give birth.

Queen, be open. It may not look how you pictured. You may be in a place that seems totally out of the ordinary, but

91

it is precisely where you must stop and allow the Queen, the Christ in you, to come forth. Be open. Let the process of Life happen, as it should. When your baby, your dream, comes forth, wrap her, keep her warm, and hold her close.

Know that she, your dream, is special, worthy, honorable, and born of God. Look for the angels' songs as the heavens proclaim the glory of your dream's birth, the God-purpose in you. Look for shepherds, who are others that get excited about your dream, to announce that the baby's coming.

But like Mary, hold these things close in your heart. Nurture your baby, your dream; care for her, protect her, and she will show you great and mighty things! Let the Queen, Christ, be born in you and through you, and bring your purpose forth.

Let there be PEACE on Earth and goodwill toward all men and in you and through you. Birth your DREAMS Queen. Let the Queen, the Christ in you, come out!

~Birthing!

Queen Reflections...

So Queen, what are you birthing? Where are you in your dream's gestation? Are you in the first trimester where no one knows but you? Are you showing? Identify where you are and wherever you are, ask God for wisdom on how to nurture and care for your dream to birth it. Write what He says to you.

DAY NINETEEN

Stop Defying Nature

Peace Queen!

Purpose comes naturally for us. It is because everything that we are called to do naturally fits into the makeup of WHO we are. It's something that often doesn't take a lot for us to do. Because of that, we can sometimes take it, purpose, for granted. Sometimes, we don't highly esteem it in the way that we should. We might even think less of it, like it's not a big deal.

I did that. For me, speaking publicly comes naturally. However, I was in a place where I was avoiding it, defying it by overlooking it and dismissing it. I reasoned that I just wanted to work with Queens one on one. I really didn't need to speak. I told myself stories as to why it was something I didn't really want to do or need to do.

Then one day, God confronted me with the Truth! He said, "Karin, if public speaking is the number one fear that most people have even beyond physical death, and you have the ability to speak publicly naturally, don't you think that is a key ingredient in the puzzle of your purpose?" DUH!! I felt a little dumbfounded.

So I knew that I had to go deeper as to WHY I was doing this, defying my nature. As I got still before the Lord, it became clear. For me, overcoming the feeling of being invisible, unimportant, and not heard as a child was at the heart of my not wanting to be fully seen and heard. There was a fear of rejection in me, still there that I was unaware of. It was because little Karin reasoned that I was unworthy of attention and was afraid of not being acceptable.

Wow! Big Karin consciously felt confident, but there was something that held me back. There was an unconscious remnant of fear still within me. So I had explained it away with the idea that I didn't want to go all over the place speaking anyway. I used the girls as my excuse saying to the Queen within, "You know, I still have younger kids," all of which was a front for fear. The funny thing is that my vision board CLEARLY shows me traveling and speaking internationally. HELLO? So what was the internal holdup? It was that childhood hangout with fear.

As I open myself up to receive the wisdom of God and went within, that's when it was revealed to me. Then I could face it, feel it, release it, and replace it. Today I say again, "I AM enough. I AM more than enough. I AM called to do great things, which are in total alignment with my natural abilities."

Speaking gives me LIFE! I'm not just good at it; I'm great at it. I'm made for this. So I've accepted it. I mentor, I coach, I write, I teach, among many other things, and I SPEAK! I AM the full package. I know the world is waiting for me. Waiting for me to say "YES."

So I say, "Yes. Here I am Lord. You can use me!" Fear falling! Faith rising in my natural purpose! No more defying it. Only accepting and flowing in it!

Queen Reflections...

Now, it's your turn. What have you been defying, avoiding, ignoring, dismissing? Why have you been doing that? This will take some excavation. Seek the Spirit. She will tell you. Face it. Feel it. Release it. Replace it. Write about it.

_____

_____

_____

_____

_____

_____

_____

_____

_____

_____

_____

_____

_____

_____

_____

_____

Karin Haysbert

DAY TWENTY

Forgive, Forget, Refocus, Move Forward

Peace Queen!

Life has a way of showing you, YOU. Well, sometimes not who you really are, but who you are masquerading as. I got some feedback that I didn't want to face. And, like so many of us, when we face an "inconvenient truth" we are offended and we get defensive. So, here I stood, trying to defend my stance, my position, my point of view, and all the while I was discounting her stance, her position, and her point of view. I heard Dr. Venus Opal Reese say this,

"Truth will set you free, but first it might insult you to your face!"

"I feel like you're holding me to the past..." she said. "What! No I'm not!" I replied knowing deep within that I really was.

I had held my sister and myself in the prison of the past. I was jailer and liberator, but first, I had to admit that I was bound. So it was the loving whisper from Mama that gently led me to the lock of my self-imposed cage.

"Read Philippians 3," Mama whispered. As my eyes scanned the chapter, I stopped at verses 13-15. "Here Dear One. This is for you."

My heart was already prepared. I had spent the preceding moments making a list of what I was thankful for about my sister and why. In my mind, I told her that I loved her and appreciated her. ...

...The key was in the lock.

Forgiveness was the fruit of that love. As love and mercy bubbled up in my heart, I forgave myself for holding her to the past.

...The key in the lock turned.

I asked her to forgive me.

...The door opened.

Now how do I walk through and not go back? "I do not count myself to have apprehended..." I humbled myself and acknowledged that we ALL miss it, me and everyone else. "But this one thing I do. Forgetting those things, which are behind."

Forgetting walks me out of the prison, never to return. Forgive and forget? But how? How do I forget what she did, what they did, what I did? It's the freeing force of forgiving and forgetting that releases it and me for good. Whatever God asks us to do, He empowers us to do. We are supreme beings. We can do whatever we intend to. I remember the lesson. I forget or release the pain. My healing is complete when it no longer hurts, when there is no sting to the memory.

Then, "reaching forward to those things which are ahead, I press toward the goal for the prize of the upward call of God in Christ Jesus." God is always calling me higher because my rewards follow me and overtake me as I ascend. So, I refocus. I cannot move forward looking backward. I focus the gaze of my heart on what I desire to see. I focus my mind on it. Visualize it. I see it inside of me. I feel it deep within my soul. What do I desire this relationship to be like?

I go up and grow up. "Therefore let us, as many as are mature, have this mind; and if in anything you think otherwise, God will reveal even this to you." When I was ready to grow up, I stopped and thought about it. As I let go and focused on my desire, the pain lifted. Now, I could move forward.

So what did I do to move forward? I called her. I told her what I had already said. "Thank you. Thank you for sharing your heart with me. Thank you for giving me a different perspective. Thank you for helping me to see what I was not seeing. I apologize for hurting or offending you. It was never my intention. Please forgive me. I love you." In that short time, years of pain were lifted, and she and I were free to move forward.

Forgive, forget, refocus, and move forward.

Queen Reflections…

Forgiveness is probably our deepest heart's work. Remember this: It's difficult to freely forgive others when you hold yourself in a prison of un-forgiveness. Start the process with you and then move outward. This may take time, but these four steps will totally free you. It's so worth the effort. Your joy and peace depend upon it. Where do you need to begin? Write about it.

For more on this chapter, go to www.queenarise.com.

_____

_____

_____

_____

_____

_____

_____

_____

_____

_____

_____

_____

_____

_____

_____

_____

DAY TWENTY-ONE

God's Coming Out

Peace Queen!

God's coming out? What!?! We think of coming out as some declaration of a hidden lifestyle that one has been secretly living. The pain becomes too great and they get enough courage to face and accept WHO they are, so now they come out to the world and say, "Here I am. Take it or leave it, but this is WHO I am."

We, through religion, have forced God to be on the "down low."

Well, in some ways, it's exactly what I mean. We, through religion, have forced God to be on the "down low." We have made it so that God's true Life has been hidden from humanity. We've placed God into boxes.

Religious boxes. Denominational boxes. "This is who God is" boxes. "This is the only way that God speaks" boxes. All kinds of boxes. We said that if you don't say it like I do, then you don't know God. We've actually made it out that God, the Almighty God, can be completely figured out by us, "treasure that is in an earthen vessel," those who "only know in part." We contain Him to books written by godly men, acting as if He began and ended in them. We've allowed it to separate us as people. We've fought about it. We've started wars over our boxes. We have killed in the name of our boxes, spiritually, physically, emotionally, relationally, and more.

Is that really what God intended? Did God mean for us to use our ways of getting to know Him as ways to disqualify others' means? Just questions to consider. Having grown up in the church, I've learned so much about who God is. I've learned a great deal about who God isn't, too. This I know for sure.

Religion is man's attempt at controlling a spiritual relationship through natural means.

God cannot be controlled or contained, and our relationship with Him cannot be either. I have learned that how I talk to God may differ from your way and that's OK. How I see God may not be how you see Him and that's OK, too. My journey to the throne is mine. I will not discount or deny yours because it is not mine. My assignment is to LOVE you so much that you see God in me, as me. As I do that, it helps you to see God in you, as you too.

My journey to the throne is mine.

That's how God's coming out: through love. Not through comparing, fussing, fighting, and condemning. Not through telling you you're wrong and I'm right, but through love, the pure essence of God Himself. So today, drop your rocks, step out of your box, open your arms, and let God come out!

Queen Reflections...

Well, well, well. Did this speak to you? How have you let religion put you in a box and close your heart to the beauty of God's love in someone else just because they didn't have the same theology as you? Go deep Queen. Search your heart. Talk with God and write.

_____

_____

_____

_____

_____

_____

_____

_____

_____

_____

_____

_____

_____

_____

_____

_____

_____

DAY TWENTY-TWO

I Need You!

Peace Queen!

I Need You!

These are three of the hardest words possibly to say. I need you. However, they are the truest words. We often see need as a sign of weakness, but recognizing the need and filling it is far from weakness. It is wisdom and it is strength.

I need air. Is it weak to need to breathe in and to breathe out? Of course not! Yet, we discount our NEED for each other.

We discount our need for each other.

I need you. This need extends far beyond faith, race, culture, gender, and even commonalities. Our need for one another is like our need for air. We are all parts of the human race. Scientists say that over 99.9% of every person on the planet is exactly the same DNA-wise, yet we concentrate vociferously on our minute differences.

I need you. When you succeed, we all succeed. I need you. When you hurt, we all hurt.

Can we open our eyes and create space in our hearts for the truth? Can we let one another in? We are all one human race. I need you. Truth is, we all need love and acceptance. We all crave community; even if we suppress it and ignore it, we still need it. The scriptures say that it is "GOOD and pleasant for us to dwell together in unity and harmony."

Especially among Queens, it's time that we acknowledge that. I say later for the shows and images that perpetuate us as not being there for one another and depicting us as catty and divisive. The generation of Queens that God is raising up knows WHO we are and that we need one another. Truth be told, we all want the same things even when we go about them in ways that are not beneficial to the whole. Sometimes from our brokenness, we try to fix it in ways that just lead to more brokenness. Cover those Queens and accept the covering when it's your turn to be covered.

Queen, I need you. I need you to arise. I need your voice in the earth. I need that special thing that God placed on the inside of you to come out so that we can all ascend from your grace and wisdom.

I need your love! Love is our common denominator. Love is the cord that binds us, and to give it or to receive it, I need you!

Queen Reflections...

Have you, in any way, discounted your need for others? Have you tried to do it all yourself? Have you isolated yourself in any way? You don't have to be alone to be isolated. You can be in the crowds and still feel lonely. How can you open up your heart to receive another Queen into your life for the up-leveling of you both? Write. Write. Write.

Karin Haysbert

DAY TWENTY-THREE

The Power of Pause for Purpose

"Be still and know that I am God."
Psalm 46:10

Peace Queen!

You're too busy—too, too busy. Going. Doing. Making it happen. Flying here. Zooming there. Pulled in 1,000 directions. And I am like the lost child in the middle of the busiest City Square. I'm looking, scanning, wondering where you are. Heart pounding, trying to see which way you went, afraid that we might never be united again. I'm wondering if this is the end of me, because you got distracted and took your eyes off of me. You weren't holding my hand and now I'm lost, or so it seems.

The one who is really lost is YOU.

110

You are lost. You're lost because you won't pause, stop, and take time to listen and really hear my voice. I AM your purpose, and we were designed to walk hand-in-hand. I actually have the blueprint. I know the way, but sometimes because I look like the lost, little girl, you feel like you need to lead me.

No! As small as I may be, if you listen to me, sit still, pause, ask me what I need to grow, and then feed it to me. I, your purpose, will expand, mature, and grow.

But, you must pause.

I've been giving you hints and clues on the trail, much like the bread crumbs that Hansel and Gretel dropped to find their way home, but your constant motion has attracted buzzards of fear that have come and eaten your bread crumbs. The once living organism called your Dream is now fading into the dying ideas, the decaying inspirations, and the decomposing visions that fear buzzards are poised to descend upon next.

I get it. You feel lost, harried, and hurried to make something happen.

"I'm getting older…

…I should be farther along than this…

…I shoulda, woulda, coulda…

…If only I hadn't…"

You fill in the blanks. All of those enslaving messages are keeping you tied to the past and wandering around the wilderness wanting rest and finding none.

Your soul is overwhelmed with trying to do it all.

Are you ready to stop? Are you ready to let go of your wilderness mindset and to release your spirit of wandering? Are you willing to finally plug into the peace of your purpose? I'm here, patiently waiting.

I'm ready to speak to you, and it all begins with pause.

Queen Reflections…

Time to evaluate. Have you been running, too? Why? What are you afraid of? Your purpose wants to speak to you and give you your next step. Perhaps, you have not followed the last directive. Get quiet. Get still. Let God breathe on you and show you your next move. Write about it.

_____

_____

_____

_____

_____

_____

_____

_____

_____

_____

_____

Karin Haysbert

DAY TWENTY-FOUR

Every Day Is My Birthday

Peace Queen!

YAY!!! It's my birthday! Today, I started this day feeling wonderful. I thought of something that I hadn't ever thought of, surprisingly. I imagined how my mother must have felt 48 years ago today. I'm sure that she was so ready to have me out of her tummy and very excited to finally see me. For the first time ever, I felt her joy in knowing that the wait to see me would soon be over. I joined her thoughts that even though it would be painful, it would be replaced with great joy of their first child, ME, being born.

It was funny to think that I had never considered that before.

Honestly, I had mostly felt the feelings of abandonment and rejection of my childhood, but today something changed on a deeper level. I had chosen to see the exuberance and anticipation of ME coming center stage into this existence and how it probably felt for my mom then. For that new perspective, I was very grateful.

Throughout the day, I only did what felt right for me. Even when my masculine side wanted to push to do something a certain way and I wobbled a bit, I quickly recovered. Even when I had opportunities to be annoyed, I wouldn't take the bait. During the times when I felt myself leaning towards being negative, I turned back to being in the vibration of love, joy, and peace. I was determined to be in sync with the Spirit and in divine alignment.

So Queen, here's my biggest BING for the day: the joy, excitement, and peace that I felt as a result of it being my birthday and receiving all of the love and blessings and good wishes from others, that is the love of God flowing through them to me. My biggest BING is that I can have that every day!

Why can't I treat every day like it's my birthday, because it is?!

Each day is a new day that we awaken into and are in essence reborn. We come into new life. We see a brand new day that we've never seen before. I want to start a revolution for my soul. I want to set a clear intention to see each day as my birthday and to celebrate it and myself as such.

You know how on your birthday you expect to receive love and well wishes and to see gifts come to you? You anticipate others singing to you and for you and about you? Isn't that what God is doing daily!? The Word says that God rejoices over us with singing. The Creator delights in ME! My maker covers and fills me with His love. The Spirit of God holds me in Her arms and tells me ALL is well.

So, today, and every day, I say to myself—HAPPY BIRTHDAY! Enjoy your very special day!

Queen Reflections...

Wow! This was a huge game changer for me. How would seeing every day as your birthday, as a joyful day that is full of joy and celebration and wonderful surprises, change your life? Write what comes up for you.

_____
_____
_____
_____
_____
_____
_____
_____
_____
_____
_____
_____
_____

Karin Haysbert

DAY TWENTY-FIVE

A Prodigal Mother?

Peace Queen!

Yesterday, I made a leap, a leap in love. It's something that I wanted to do but was afraid to allow myself to do. Yesterday, I went into a deeper dimension of love.

Loving and accepting my son, just the way he was, on the way to where he's going has been a challenge, to say the least. It was challenging because I have had glimpses of his greatness. It's been a struggle for me because I have resented his struggle. Imagine that?

I judged his journey.

I measured his life by my own and I didn't want to accept that there were really good reasons for everything that he's done or not done. I didn't want to allow him to find his own way so that I could disconnect from the pain and disappointment.

118

Here's what I wanted. I wanted to end the pain by simply telling him which road to take in order to stop the madness that swirled around him and within him. I wanted to silence the lying voices that had led him astray. I wanted to relieve him because it would relieve me. Getting him straight would validate me. It would, in my mind, release me from my connection to his hurt and exonerate me. Release me from any responsibility for it. But that's not how it goes.

Everybody was sent here to learn their own lessons and to forge their own way.

Although we all have help along the way, we must each grapple with life's joys and sorrows and find our true selves, by ourselves. No one can forge a relationship with God for you. As my father often says, "God only has children. He doesn't have grandchildren." Everyone has his or her own hero's journey.

So, I finally let go, or so I thought. That's what I told myself months ago. Truth is, I pulled over, and like a taxi driver reaching her destination to let my son out of my emotional car but like a cabbie, I was looking for a fare.

"You need to pay me for where I drove you. Pay me by doing what I think is right for you. If you don't give me the fare, I won't open the door."

What I didn't realize then was that my withholding love was like me being the driver refusing to open the car's door, demanding a fare. It was keeping my son trapped in my emotional car. It's false imprisonment! I was keeping him and myself in a cage of fear. Fear that he might not get it. Fear that I'll feel like a terrible mother, a prodigal mother if he never comes back home. Fear that he may never come to himself. Fear that the pain of disappointment may never go away.

But LOVE kept calling.

Love was the key that unlocked the doors. It opened my heart to simply accept him. It empowered me to set us both free. Love made me able to see the good in it all and to get things from his perspective. Love brought me back to the Father and his lavish love.

Sometimes we look at others thinking that they are the prodigal, but in truth our judgment and disdain for their journey shows who the prodigal really is.

So today, I rejoice because not only am I at a deeper level of love in my Father's House of Love, but that my son is coming to himself and coming home, too. Yes, prodigals do come home.

Thank you! Thank you! Thank you!

Queen Reflections...

Alrighty Queen. How about you? Where do you need to come back to the Father's love in your life? Is there any place in your life where you have stood in judgment of another's journey that you simply need to love and accept them and to let go? Surrender. Write. Write. Write. Let God reveal the Truth.

Karin Haysbert

DAY TWENTY-SIX

Taking My Power Back!
OCTOBER 2, 2015

Peace Queen!

I'm telling you up front. This one is raw for me. It was a snapshot in time, and things often do change. Why did I give away my power? When did it slip from my grasp? After my quarter-life crisis and I had begun to stand up for myself. I had freed myself from an abusive relationship with my son's father. I had begun to see myself as valuable and had stopped abusing myself. I had started to feel confident again. I was abundant. I felt stronger. But the crossroad came when I knew deep within myself that what I was doing professionally was unfulfilling. It paid the bills, but I didn't love it. I didn't even like it that much. I was just doing what I felt that I "had to do." Sometimes "obligations" can be fatal to purpose. I knew that I felt led to empowering women, to speaking life into their souls, to giving them what I felt I needed, but I didn't see how other women would listen to me, even though I knew I was called to them.

Why? I was young. I was a single mother who had finally escaped a mentally, physically, and emotionally abusive relationship with my son's father. I loved God. I loved His Word. I knew that there was a great deal of wisdom in me from my walk with God and from overcoming my trials and tribulations, but I despised my youth and I was deeply ashamed of my "mistakes." I still had more healing to do myself.

I felt like damaged goods.

I did have many things going for myself. I was pretty independent. I owned my own house at 24 and I owned my own car, fully paid for. I had plenty of money in the bank and was making good money. I looked successful on the outside by society's standards, but something inside of me was saying, "No, this isn't it." I felt restless within my soul. I knew I was supposed to teach. Maybe that's it! Maybe I'm a schoolteacher?

I left corporate America and took a very entry-level job as an assistant teacher at a middle school after substitute teaching for a while. At least I was not afraid to jump. While there was some reward in working with students and special education students in particular, that still wasn't it. I knew there was a call, but I just couldn't see how I could fulfill it.

I was tired. No, I was exhausted! I was feeling the weight of having to "do it all" without the clarity of how to bring my gifts forward. I wanted relief. I needed rest. I craved the joy and comfort of a relationship. It created the perfect storm.

The voices whispered, "A man is supposed to take care of you. God made man and took Eve out of him. He'll be your head. He'll be responsible for you. A godly man will love you like Christ loves the Church. He will provide for you and protect you and lay down his life for you. All you have to do is love and submit to him. God will bless that! Get yourself a godly man. A 'Knight in Shining Armor.'"

Now, let's be clear. Hindsight is 20/20. Did I realize the many programs running through my mind? Not entirely, but this is what I heard church folks say. Sounds good, right? A godly man will love you and take care of you and be your "everything." I know what I grew up with. I grew up seeing parents who were together and who never fought, at least not in front of us. I saw a mom who handled EVERYTHING at home AND worked outside of the home. She had a cape flying from her back. From what I could see, that's how it worked, or was supposed to work. They seemed happy enough. They were together when other less "spiritual" family members had split. So in my mind that was how it was supposed to be. My parents were doing it "God's way," I thought.

So, I sought after the perfect man for me. He was to be a godly man, who loved God, my son, and me and would do what the Word taught. And I proceeded to be the perfect woman for him. I was a godly woman, who loved God and him. I did what they said, "Follow him," even if it felt like it took us nowhere at times. I "submitted." I kept my mouth shut. I waited for him to stand up and to be the "head," to take control and to lead us, just like they told me to. I stopped doing things that I would normally just handle. I was waiting for him to be all that I made him out to be.

I wanted him to approve of me and to affirm who I was and what I wanted to do. It was almost as if I were a child again. I was so afraid of doing it, marriage, wrongly. It paralyzed me. That little girl in me, who felt so much rejection and maybe all of the little girls from generations before too, huddled within and waited and waited and waited…for validation… for permission…to BE.

I went along to get along and betrayed myself.

Now, don't get me wrong, I have a great husband. He did the very best that he could. This is not about him at all. It's about me and me not living up to the life that God placed on the inside of ME. This is about my not standing in my own power and not feeling worthy to speak my own truth regardless of fear.

It didn't change until I looked myself in the eye one day and got real, raw, and honest with myself. I had to admit that I was doing exactly what I had despised about what I had finally seen in the lives of women around me. These were women who were close to me who I looked up to. Women who are powerhouses. Women who are strong, wise, loving, and giving. What I had to realize was that perhaps these beautiful Queens were living from the little girls within them and were simply afraid of rejection and disapproval, too. What a paradox for us strong, capable women. My heart broke as I observed these carriers of light cut off their light, not just dim it, but cut it off so that others wouldn't feel threatened. In some cases, I felt like I witnessed Queens losing their essence and spark by trying to please others, and men in particular, who seem so inconsolable with themselves at times that nothing these Queens said or did was ever enough anyway. I watched mothers, daughters, aunties, sisters, and friends deny their dreams in the process and strangle their purpose—all but turning their backs on them. I saw myself in these Queens.

Rage rose within me. No more!

I've seen Queens struggling, dying on the vine in dry and thirsty places, wanting so much more for themselves and their walk with God—but afraid to move on so as not to appear "unsubmitted." "You're supposed to be with your husband wherever he is at church," folks say. I've watched powerful women of God whose own souls shriveled because they were simply out of place and the gifts within them had not been truly stirred in so long that they had almost become stagnant. Every now and then, a sign of life would surface only to be snuffed out by the suffocating insecurity of those they allowed to keep them captive. It doesn't make the insecure "captors" bad people. They are just broken people who often deny their own wounds. Casting blame and playing the victim has become a familiar friend because they're just deceived and need someone else to control in order to feel in control of themselves.

Deception is deadliest when swallowed by the person serving it. So is denial.

So, I've watched for years what appears to me as the slow death of Queens within my arm's reach. Women whom I love. Women whom I care for. Women whom I respect and look up to. Women who deserve so much more! It's a painful, torturous wrenching of the soul's purpose draining away. Life fleeting. Like the woman with the issue of blood who was losing life, no one else could help them. Only they could help themselves when they reach out in faith to touch Christ for their own wholeness. But like Jesus often asked, "Do you want to be healed?" Do you want to be free?

I WANTED TO BE FREE!

I did! I realized that looking at them, I was seeing a reflection of myself. Once I clearly saw fear's imprisonment and the path of passivity that I was walking on, my answer was YES! I said later for the vicissitude of victimhood, I wanted to be free. So, one step at a time, I began to straighten up, to stand up, and

126

to square my shoulders. I began to acknowledge WHO I am. I began to assert that God made me who I am and no one else can or needs to validate that. I learned from these other Queens' journeys and my own that I am accountable to God for myself alone. I'm responsible for myself. Certainly I play a part in everyone else's life, but if I work on clearing my own faulty programs, that is to remove my own "mote," then I can see clearly to help others to remove their "specks."

The generations of women being bound by needing men to give them permission to BE stops here.

I transform myself so I can leave a legacy of "Queens Arising" for my lineage to follow in. I set the exiled Queen within me free and return her to her throne. I take my power back. I make my own choices. I follow my own leading. I stand in agreement with others as the Spirit leads. I no longer just go along to get along. My divine destiny's fulfillment is in my answering my call to greatness. It's not in waiting to see if anyone else will. The Queens are indeed rising.

We're saying that true submission is submission to God.

When I'm submitted to God and please the Father, that's enough. All things are right in line. So I no longer sit by the metaphorical pool of Bethesda waiting for someone to put me into it. I take my healing into my own hands. I stand up, get into position, and dive into the river of life headfirst, swimming into the center of my stream.

I take my power back and arise!

Queen Reflections...

Well. Well. Well. Did this tug at your heart? Have you dimmed your light out of fear of rejection? Have you been hiding behind being "submitted" waiting for someone, anyone else, to validate what God has already told you? Other Queens need you to step up, not just for yourself, but so that you can show them what is possible. I'm so happy and thankful to say that some of those same Queens who I have watched over the years have begun to truly awaken and blossom and step into their purpose now and take a stand for themselves as I have. It is never too late to begin again. Step up. Step out. Take your power back! Time to get very real Queen. Write!

For more on this chapter, go to www.queenarise.com.

Karin Haysbert

DAY TWENTY-SEVEN

Receiving My Good

Peace Queen!

I am a giver, but NOW (right now) I open myself up to being a bigger receiver. What I sow by Law, I reap IF (and "if" is the operative word) I can and will receive it. So in order for me to receive the 30-, 60-, 100-, 1,000-fold, I must expand my capacity to receive. That is, I must enlarge my mental territory and lengthen my mind's chords. I must open my heart to believe!

It's waiting. The blessings are waiting in the heavens to come to me. When I open the door of my heart and mind through loving and having good feelings about what it is that I desire, my money, my prosperity, my blessings can come to me. I realize now that I cannot have that which I do not feel worthy of receiving. I cannot have what I don't feel and believe that I deserve.

Negative thoughts, feelings, words, and beliefs about money or wealth repel our blessings, regardless of whether we tithe or give. We override the Law with unbelief.

"Now He did not do many mighty works there because of their unbelief."
Matthew 13:58

There were places where Jesus could not do miracles because of their unbelief. The miracles of money, prosperity, and blessings will only flow to belief. We're told that we cannot love God and mammon. We are to love God, love people, and to use money. We are the masters. Money is the servant.

Money is merely a tool that we use in order to exchange value. Although we do not love money, we should love what money can do for us. Are you serious? Money is supposed to be used to spread love and good feelings throughout the world. Yes. I love that!

Queen, money is a neutral force, and it can be used for all kinds of purposes. When we use it for the sake of love, it is added without sorrow. We can receive it, riches, added to us without hard toil. (Proverbs 10:22)

So today, flow in love and open up to receive all of the good that God has for you!

Receiving!

Queen Reflections...

So Queen, are you a good receiver? How is your relationship with money? Do you feel worthy of the blessings of God? What do you need to shift in your thinking to receive? Write about it.

For more on this chapter, go to www.queenarise.com.

Karin Haysbert

DAY TWENTY-EIGHT

What a Common Cold Taught Me

Peace Queen!

Here's what I know for sure... What we're here to learn, we are here to teach. So, the life lesson that I master is the lesson I minister. I wrote about the evaporation of confusion a little while ago. Well, here comes a pop quiz to see if I really got the message.

Too much happening at once. Too many voices. Confusion!

How it manifested was in a cold. I almost never get colds, and it seemed to happen at a most inopportune time; however, learning and growth are Kairos moments that take place when we are ready to receive them. Hence, they are always at the right time! Here I am God. Show me.

First, I was spreading myself too thin! I cannot do it all. I know this consciously. I didn't even feel like I was doing that, but I know that Spirit is saying again, "Simplify!" Remove clutter. Unsubscribe to the dozens of lists that you are on. Pick one book to read. Set clear boundaries with regard to your time.

Secondly, self-care. Get out in nature. Go for a walk. Listen to the raindrops. Watch the clouds go by. Sit in silence. Do nothing. Get an ice cream sundae. Get your nails done. Go to a movie. Laugh. Dance. Sing. Play. Get a massage. Read a fiction book. Let go. Take a bubble bath. Take care of YOU!

Thirdly, decide to feel good no matter what. Stop negative thoughts immediately. Open your mouth and speak Truth. Talk about what's good, what you learned, and what you're so grateful for. Change your state. Stay in a "feel-good zone" at all costs. Get into the vibration of goodness and stay there. Create from that place.

Fourthly, LOVE. Focus on what you love, who you love, and all that love gives to you. Look for ways to express love and appreciation all throughout the day. Decide to walk in love and compassion towards yourself and others.

Fifthly, honesty. Be honest with yourself about what you desire. Be clear about what works for you. Be courageous enough to "speak the Truth in love" to yourself and to others.

Sixth, ease. Release the notion that things have to be so hard. They will not always be easy, but that is only because we have to let go of so many false beliefs. We hold onto them so tightly that they have been ingrained in us. To release them, it's almost like a tearing away. That can make it feel hard. However, if we will loosen our grip, it can flow away easily. It doesn't have to be so hard.

I hear the Spirit's sweet voice saying, "Come unto me all you who are weary"... weary of fighting... weary of making life so hard..." and I will give you rest." Rest in God's goodness. It's fully available to us, if we will just receive it.

"Take my yoke upon you and learn of me..." Link up to Me and see how I walked as Christ. I didn't struggle and fight. I asked, I believed, and I received. I decreed and I declared. And it was so! The same power to be, do, and have is in us all.

"For I am meek and lowly in heart...." I am Strength under control. I am disciplined, diligent, and decisive. I operate my life according to God's laws of the universe. I humble myself to them.

And when you do, "you shall find rest for your soul!" Your mind and heart will be clean, clear, and at peace...in rest.

So today, I go back to my schedule and take half of it out. I inject lots of love, joy, peace, and play into it. I put in things that delight me. I let go of some things and I embrace others. I gain clarity and restore my spiritual, mental, emotional, and then physical health. Since my body speaks my mind, I listen to her voice and heed the lessons.

Wow! I can feel the "cold" leaving me now as I warm up to myself. Selah!

Queen Reflections…

How about you? I learned quite a bit from that cold. Which lessons spoke to you? How will you simplify your life and warm up to yourself? Write it out!

_____

_____

_____

_____

_____

_____

_____

_____

_____

_____

_____

_____

_____

_____

_____

_____

_____

_____

_____

_____

DAY TWENTY-NINE

Stand Up and Tell the Truth!

Peace Queen!

Years ago when I was a little girl, there was a TV game show called "To Tell the Truth." The show had a panel of celebrity guests whose objective was to correctly identify the described contestant. The celebrities interviewed contestants, the real person and two imposters, to try to identify who was the real person. At the end of the game the host would ask the million-dollar question: "Would the real Karin Haysbert please stand up?" And interestingly enough, there were times when you would hit it right on the head, but then there were times when you were way off. Maybe some of those imposters were really actors.

Why did we like that show? It aired successfully for many years. Do we enjoy the challenge of trying to figure out WHO someone really is? Maybe it's the excitement of seeing whether or not we can tell if someone is lying or not. Whatever the case, we all need to play a little game of "To Tell the Truth" with ourselves.

Who are you? No, who are you really? Just like those three contestants in the game show, there are often three versions of ourselves. The first one is the one who we show to everyone else. It is the Pretend Self. She fits into all of the "right" places. She says what she is supposed to say. She does what she is supposed to do. She's crafted after society's mold. You may be able to get by with her for a while, but in time the voice of your Real Self cries out in your wilderness for freedom and will not be hidden.

Then there's the Self that We Think We Are. This self is what we really think about ourselves, consciously. It's probably the self that we hide from others for fear of judgment or rejection. But in truth, this self is probably getting closer to our Real Self, although she is not entirely our Real Self. The perspective of the programs that are running inside of and around our Real Self alter her into seeing ourselves in this limited way. These voices hinder her from reaching her fullest potential. They whisper lies to her, and as she accepts some of the lies as truth, they become "truth" for her. They become her reality. The Self that We Think We Are spends way too much time majoring on the minors. She wants more but doesn't know how to get to it.

Then there's the Real Self, the real you. The Real You is treasure in an earthen vessel. This is the Divine You, the Queen. This is the you who can do ALL things through Christ. The Real You loves fully, gives freely, and easily receives. She is perfection in flesh. What we often fail to accept is that we really are perfect beings. We simply do not always express perfectly. The imperfect expression comes from the fears that ensnare the Self that We Think We Are. The Real You knows your power and constantly urges you to renew your mind so that the Real You can emerge.

Now, just like in that wonderful game show, we've got to find the Real Self, the Real You. We must begin to ask ourselves some deep questions. Let's get curious Queens! We've got to start to sift through the stuff we put on to please others and the things we've held ourselves back from because of her own fears and anxieties. We've got to get to the root of the matter, the core of who we really are. From that place of royalty and Divinity, we can then build while we release all that is not the real "us."

So today, take some time to get to know the Real You—the Bold You, the Fearless You, the Loving You, the Strong You, the Complete You, the Perfect You, the Queen You. And when you ask, "Will the Real You please stand up?" Stand up! Queen arise!

Queen Reflections...

So are you ready to SEE the Real You, The Queen within. I'm sure that you are seeing more and more of her already as you go through this process. What is something that you are ready to release and something that you are ready to embrace? (Really take your time in the extra space that has been provided.)

Karin Haysbert

DAY THIRTY

Pray Without Ceasing!

Peace Queen!

Mama's love never ceases. The Spirit of God always wants to show Her love for me, to me, and through me. She has so much to say to bring about the beautiful life that she and the Father had planned for me—if only I would stop to listen to it, take time to hear Her sweet voice, and settle into times alone where She and I can commune. It's here that I see Her and realize that I am a reflection of Her. I am made in God's image.

I reflect God's glory.

Flesh, ego, the world's way of thinking tells me the opposite. It tells me that because I did wrong, I am wrong. It says that because I made a mistake, I am a mistake. It wants me to wallow in self-pity, defeat, guilt, shame, and condemnation. It wants to keep me controlled, the same, and "safe" in a twisted way, so that it knows what to expect.

That is so counter to who I am. Me, the real Me, loves the thrill of newness, the excitement of the unexpected, the magnificence of "Wow, what else could happen?!" This is a life of growth, expansion, and unfolding. It's a journey of going from glory to glory. I can only achieve this life of joy as I am connected to my Divine Source. This connection is through prayer.

PRAYER!

Prayers of praise. Prayers of thanksgiving. Petition prayers. Breath prayers. Supplications. Pissed prayers. Angry prayers. Hopeful prayers. Written prayers. Prayers that I sing. Silent prayers.... Whatever kind of prayer it is, Mama knows my heart and my mind, and she wants to let the mind of Christ be in me. As I reach out, She reaches in and I am transformed.

Just like I need breath in order for my body to live, I need prayer for my spirit, the real me, the Queen within to thrive.

Pray. Pray. Pray Without Ceasing!

Queen Reflections...

So how's your connection, Queen? Do you pray without ceasing? I believe that we need a set time when we pray, but we also need free-flowing continuous conversations with the Christ within. Write what this means to you.

DAY THIRTY-ONE

Unshackled Sexuality

Peace Queen!

Making love! Doing it! SEX!! We all want it; well most of us do. We all NEED it! Now, that's true. We're all here because of it. OK, we can all agree on that (smiles). Suffice it to say, it is a central part of WHO we are. But somehow sex for me had become sullied, dirty, shameful, and painful.

"I have been delivered!

From what? ... None of your business! That's between God and me. Some things should go with you to the grave," he said.

That's what my pastor at the time told us that we should say. What he was really telling us is that we should hide our pain, conceal our struggles, and never ask for help. Fake it 'til you make it. That's how I heard it.

"You're a leader. What are you doing at the altar?" he chided. I heard, "You better not show yourself. Nobody needs to know about you and your business. Not even your spouse."

What I didn't know was that these were the words of a wounded man who wanted to hide himself. He was living more than a double-life, and because of my own shame I swallowed it all, hook, line, and sinker.

I swallowed my shame. I swallowed my fear. I swallowed the feeling that I was "damaged goods" and that if anyone really knew my story that they wouldn't accept me or no one would really want me.

So here I was, pretending the pain did not exist. I put on my "Praise the Lords." I looked holy, righteous, sanctified, and whole.

When the flower is forced to open its petals before the appointed time, there will be consequences, often-negative consequences.

Flashback! ... When an older "family member" introduced me to a "fun game that would feel really good," I was in. Besides, he was like a big brother to me. I was a lonely, only child and looked up to him. It didn't involve intercourse. It was a "humping game" fully clothed, but sometimes not.

A desire was awakened.

And since it was a game, and it was fun, I told other people about it in my naïveté. It was just a part of my summer fun, or so I thought.

The next summer, when I saw my "big brother" again, I was ready for the game. But he was not. What I didn't know was that from one year to the next, it seems that he had gone to the next level in the game, the next world. He was much more interested in carrying out the next level game with a cousin of mine. This cousin was light-skinned, with light eyes, and long hair. I felt so rejected, not good enough, and not pretty enough. I didn't realize it then, but God was protecting me.

What I saw as rejection was really protection.

I thought I was rejected because I was darker, had short hair, and those "big Bubba lips," the phrase bullies used to tease me with. I thought I was not beautiful. Rejection took a firm hold of my soul. That's why he doesn't want to play the game with me! From then on, the lively, gregarious, little girl retreated. I became quiet, I became shy, and low self-esteem became a dangling noose around my neck. I couldn't get too far from it, or it would choke me and pull me back.

At the same time, we moved back to Baltimore from the DC area, where my father began a new job and took on another church assignment. In DC, he at least spent some time with me, but here in Baltimore, all he did was work.

I withdrew more. My mom never seemed to connect with me on an emotional level. I shrank more. My parents had another child and she got all of the attention. I sank even deeper into the pain, reeling in my perceived rejection.

I've always been a reader. Going through my dad's library, I came across some old medical journals. At one time, he was studying to be a medical doctor. In the journal, I saw a picture of a young girl around my age who was pregnant! Oh my God, could I be pregnant?! I was ignorant of the facts of life. Fear gripped me. I went to the public library in my neighborhood and researched more. That's how I found out what sex was. "OH! I'm not pregnant," I thought, "but I am still damaged and dirty."

Deep SHAME entered my heart.

I should have never done this "humping game." It's not a game at all. It's my fault. I played this game and told others about it, too. I'm a terrible person. That is how I felt.

Then, over the years, sex became the forbidden fruit that everyone wants but you are not supposed to have—that is, unless you are married. Well, I wasn't married and I had sex. I had sex to feel loved. I had sex to feel wanted. I had sex to have a boyfriend. I didn't do it much, but enough to swim in a sea of shame.

Time passed. I grew. I matured. I began to see sex as a gift. It was a gift I wanted to share with my future spouse, but I still pushed the boundaries from time to time. Sex is something that you should never have to say, "No," to, but when you skirt around the edges after making a decision to wait, you make your body say, "No," to what it's designed to say, "Yes," to. That is called "playing with fire." You will get burned! Then when we get married, we think our bodies will automatically say, "Yes." It didn't happen that way for me.

I was so bound by my past shame and guilt and enslaved by the "submission omissions," you know the stuff that folks left out of the story of submission, that for almost two decades, I waited and waited and waited for my husband to give me permission to be free sexually. He couldn't. It was only mine to give.

So, I gave myself permission.

I gave myself permission through forgiveness. I forgave myself for every sexual mistake because I know that it was a deeper issue.

It was shame.
It was guilt.
It was the fear of rejection.
It was the fear of being unlovable.
It was the fear of never being loved.

I forgave everyone who violated me and for my violation of others. I forgave myself for what I did knowingly and for that which was done without knowledge. I realized that the past is over, and I refused to allow it to tie me to a grindstone of guilt.

I decided to live my sexual life unshackled. I gave myself the freedom to explore the heights of pleasure and the depths of desire. It is God's gift to me. It's my gift to myself...to be free...really free in unshackled sexuality.

Queen Reflections...

There are two times when some of us get really quiet, especially "church folks"—when we talk about money and when we talk about sex. Don't be quiet anymore. What comes up for you here? Has guilt and shame kept you from living unshackled sexually? Write about it. God wants you to be FREE! Free to enjoy this unspeakable gift.

For more on this chapter, go to www.queenarise.com.

DAY THIRTY-TWO

FREE!

Peace Queen!

Balance, Simplicity, Harmony, Freedom...

I crave it from the depths of my soul. I don't want to feel pushed and pulled or compelled. I want to feel that I'm stretching, reaching, and propelled. Propelled into my purpose. Grounded, secure, and connected.

Fear makes us grab instead of reach. We grab for whatever is close, whatever seems easy, whatever will be a temporary fix. Fear makes us vulnerable to the trail of temptation. The object of temptation, in and of itself, is not bad. Who doesn't want to be happy, to feel excitement, to be aware of their aliveness and all of the brilliance of life? Everyone does! Temptation shows you what you really want, which is usually a good thing, but with a twist in how you get it. The trail of temptation offers a crooked path, a shortcut, to the often-good thing.

When fear motivates us, we jump onto temptation's trail because it seems easier. It is not. The problem is its trappings

153

are temporary. We may get it, but we can't keep it. How we get what we desire is often more important than the desire itself. The power is in the process—that is, WHO we become in the desire's attainment.

"There is a way that seems right to a man, but its end is death."
– Separation from God, detachment from love, security, safety, and peace.

Everything we get on the trail of temptation, we are afraid we'll lose. "Stolen water is sweet and bread eaten in secret is pleasant," says the way of folly, the form of the fearful, but "the dead are there."

We cannot be alive to God and live in the clutches of fear, desperately seizing whatever comes. It's a decoy. The path leads to destruction. So again, BALANCE me Lord. Let my thoughts be weighed on your divine scale. When my thoughts are placed on one side and yours for me on any matter are on the other side, may they be level, even in HARMONY.

Help me to SIMPLIFY my life, to cut away the excess, the things I use to distract myself to take me away from the direction to my destiny. Empower me to "lay aside the sin," the ways I miss the mark you set for me, "and the weights," things I've picked up knowingly or unknowingly that divert me and sidetrack me. I lay all of those burdens down and come to You, with You, to my place in You, the place you carved out for me before you said, "Let there be" because I always was in You.

Sustain me Lord as I go on this journey to all you have appointed to me, unencumbered, free of worry, free of fear...

FREE!

Queen Reflections...

OK, Queen. Be honest. What is tempting you right now? What is trying to take you off of your game, out of your place in God? What do you need to cut away? Who do you need to delete from your life? What do you have to do to be FREE? Write what comes up for you?

_____
_____
_____
_____
_____
_____
_____
_____
_____
_____
_____
_____
_____

DAY THIRTY-THREE

When Loving You Is Hurting Me, It's Time to Go!

"To everything there is a season
and a time to every purpose under the heaven."
Eccles. 3:1

Peace Queen!

Letting go can be challenging, especially if you have a great emotional investment into a person or project and you really, really love them or it. However, when loving you is hurting me, I might need to release you (which is really releasing myself). I encountered this with a very close friend recently. I knew in my heart that I had to let her go, but I wrestled with it for years.

Then, like God often does, He allowed a circumstance to arise totally out of left field in which case she mistook something that caused her to distance herself from me. What? Even though I knew that it was time and I still sought to explain to her that she, in fact, was not correct in her assumption about me, it didn't negate the truth. It was TIME to move on. However true, it also didn't eliminate the pain of letting go. Here's what came up for me...

I love you. I really, really love you, but I love me more. Loving you should not hurt me. Now, I realize that sometimes there is pain, but it cannot be our relationship's mantra.

Trust.

It's a word that means so many things to as many people. Trust is the internal fiber upon which any intimate relationship is built. Trust is born out of love that has been expressed and received consistently. Trust is the foundation of "ease" in a relationship. It doesn't mean that either party will always do things "right," but it does mean that even when we miss it, there are enough emotional deposits to stand upon.

Where there is no trust, there is no healthy, intimate relationship.

Truth is, if there is little or no trust, loving you is hurting me. It hurts me more than it heals me. So, as a result of following love, I, in order to love me more, have to release you.

It makes no difference if the trust has waned with me or with you. I make a decision to love and trust myself so much that I'm willing to move on to see what new horizons can be arranged in the skyline of my life. Each day is a brand-new start. I awaken to new possibilities with each rising sun. I accept that there's so much love waiting for me to embrace but knowing that nothing new gets into a closed hand or a closed heart. So today,

**I let go of what was,
I open up to what is,
and I allow my grand future to unfold...**

still loving you, but letting go by loving me more!

ALL people are in your life for a reason.

Most people are in your life for a season.

Few people are in your life for a lifetime.

It's OK to let go! Queen, I hope that helps you on your journey. Be true to yourself. Release and let go! Greater love awaits you! Receive it!

Queen Reflections...

How about you, Queen? Is there a person, a project, a thought, or a belief that you have held onto way beyond its expiration date? Search your heart. Know that God, the unlimited God, will never ask you to release anything or anyone unless He has better awaiting you. Write about it.

DAY THIRTY-FOUR

The Stage Play of Life

Peace Queen!

Take 100% responsibility for how your life is right now.

What? One hundred percent? Yes! One hundred percent responsibility! Why are we more willing to take one hundred percent responsibility or credit for success yet very unwilling, many times, to take a little if any responsibility for our perceived "failures"? We can so quickly blame others—our parents, our upbringing, the mean kids at school, and the person who hurt me, betrayed me, or violated me. We blame the devil and even God.

Yet, when we look at all of the experiences of our lives, we always find ourselves there.

Wherever you go, there YOU are. The greatest common factor is... drumroll... YOU!!! It's me! I'm the actor. I'm the producer. And, although I may not want to accept it, I'm also the playwright. Do you know why?

There is something in me that set the stage for everything happening in my life.

Whatever it is. Ouch! That hurts sometimes. So, am I to blame? No, I wouldn't take on the energy or the shame of blame. I will, however, adjure you to take full responsibility for how you act in life's lessons now. You are responsible for how you respond to them.

But what if I can't explain what in me caused it to appear? Do you really need to?

By taking responsibility for it coming, you have also empowered yourself to let it go. I brought it here. It's here and I can send it packing.

BE GONE!

I can let it go by choosing thoughts and feelings in alignment with my true heart's desire, the thoughts of the Queen within. I can create a new situation for me based on love and not fear. I can fully embrace all of the wonderful possibilities and opportunities and then release the limitations.

I can write a new play.

I can have fun and play my way to what I want. I can realize that I am a divine creative being fully capable of making a new life for myself by leaning into the love and life that God already provided for me. I can fall into fun and allow the blessed path to unfold for me. I can reset the stage play of my life into the one that I've dreamed of and birth it into my present reality.

Yes, I AM one hundred percent responsible for my life. So, how I respond right now is by taking my place, center stage, raising the curtain on my life and letting a new play begin. ~Queen arise!

Queen Reflections...

So Queen, are you ready for a new story, a new outlook for your life to unfold? What do you need to take responsibility for so that you can write a new play and let the Queen arise in you? Once you do, all you will need to do is hop onstage and act it out. Write what comes up for you.

_____

_____

_____

_____

_____

_____

_____

_____

_____

_____

_____

DAY THIRTY-FIVE

Learning the Delicate Art of Delegation

Peace Queen!

Queen, why are you trying to do it all? You're overwhelmed. You're frustrated. You're at your wit's end. I was reading Exodus 18 today and came across a powerful truth.

Delegation. If I could subtitle this, I would also call it, "You need me, don't you?" Moses's father-in-law, Jethro, came to visit him. The next day, Moses took his seat to serve as judge for the people. Side-note:

Anytime you sit to judge people, it will wear YOU out.

I'm back. Moses would hear matters and bring resolution to controversies, but he did this from morning until evening. Jethro questioned him and told him...

"What you are doing is not good. You and these people will only wear yourselves out. It's too heavy to do alone."

As I meditated on this passage, I found a few reasons why we try to do it ALL alone.

First, we may have been taught to do just that. I grew up seeing my mother do it all. She worked full-time outside of the home and then did everything, and I do mean everything in the home, too. To me, that was normal. The wife "should" be keeper of the home and take care of just about everything concerning it. OK. But if you work full-time outside of the home, just like your husband, why does he get to clock out at home from work while you get to clock in at home to another full-time job? It didn't add up, but that was all I knew.

I wasn't accustomed to seeing a couple that shares the distribution of labor in the home. I thought I was being a "good, submissive wife" by doing it all. I quickly became worn out, angry, and resentful. I directed it in my mind towards my husband, who seemed clueless about my overload, but it was really towards myself. I sat day and night handling virtually everything, like Moses, and I wouldn't ask for help. That was on me. I never saw my mother ask for help, so neither did I. It was NOT working.

Secondly, sometimes we try to do it all because, deep within, we have a "need to be needed" in an unbalanced way. We make everything have to come through us because we're lacking in self-esteem or our sense of self-worth has been compromised. We want to be seen as the "go-to person" because it validates us. It makes us feel good if others need us or they can't do something without us. Their dependency is our pay for the wear-out.

My third reason for why we sometimes try to do it all is because we do not trust. Often, we don't trust others because we don't feel that we can trust ourselves. We may have been told not to trust anyone but God, not even ourselves. That's what they told me in church. They said, "People will fail you. Only trust God." Really? So how do you have a sound relationship without trust? Yes, I trust God, but I'm always trusting God when I trust anyone else because I'm trusting in the God in them. I'm not trusting in their carnal nature, their ego, or their fears. Truth is, you cannot live life alone. It just doesn't work that way. You and I are part of the whole. We are necessary parts of God on Earth, and we do need each other. Trust is the lifeblood of our intimate relationships.

So Jethro gave Moses some divine wisdom. First, He told Moses to:

TEACH the people God's decrees and SHOW them how to live them.

Queen, stop making people depend on you for the answers so that you can feel needed or like the Queen Bee. Teach people to go within and get their own answers. Show people how to know God for themselves. Let people have their journeys. Get out of the way. Let people grow up.

Secondly,

Get help!

Put a team of capable people around you. Let go. Release the reins. Give them the authority and the ability to handle matters that are not essential for you to do. Stop doing things that you don't personally need to do. Stop being busy, and be effective and efficient. Activity does not mean you were getting things done. Streamline through delegation.

The load becomes so much lighter when you share it.

Thirdly, stay in your area of expertise. Once you have let go and trusted things to others' care, focus on doing ONLY what you are uniquely qualified and gifted to do. Jethro told Moses, "If you do this and so command, you will be able to withstand the strain and all the people will go home satisfied."

Go deeper Queens. Ask yourself: Why are you trying to do it ALL on your own? It's OK to let go. Needing or asking for help is not a sign of weakness. It's a sign of great wisdom and strength. No Queen is an island. You're meant to reign among a Queendom of many of Queens.

You do your part. Let others do their part, and trust God for the best outcome.

So, today scrape some things off of your plate. Someone's empty plate needs your serving. Delegate!

Queen Reflections...

OK, Queen. This may take a while. I want you to really take a moment to evaluate why you have held onto things that you should have released long ago? Why haven't you? Let's clear that up or you may end up right back at the same place. Go deeper. Make a list of what's in your area of genius and what is not. What can you delegate to another. What is it worth for you to pay someone else to do because your time is more valuable? Think deeply about this and start delegating, you wise and strong Queen! Write!

Karin Haysbert

DAY THIRTY-SIX

Say Hello to Peace

Peace Queen!

I've been declaring peace to you each day. But, what is peace? Let's start with what it is not.

Peace is not the absence of strife.
Peace is not the elimination of stressful events.
Peace is not even the calming of the storm around you.

How about what peace is?

Peace is, however, the calming of the storm within you.
Peace is the harmonious assurance that no matter what,
all things are indeed working together for your highest
good.
Peace is wholeness and soundness.
Peace is nothing missing and nothing broken.
Peace is prosperity.
That's what God's peace is.

171

Queen, can you believe that? If you can, and you can, you can have the peace that passes all understanding. It is a confidence that God has you no matter what.

Years ago during my trip in the pigpen of life, I discovered that I needed to go back home to the Father because of the absence of peace. Here's what He told me. Peace is the:

P—PATIENT

E—EXPECTATION OF GOD

A---ACTING

C---CONCLUSIVELY IN

E---EVERY AREA OF MY LIFE

That's the peace of God. I am patient, enduring without complaint, focused on the good, with an expectation! I have great hope that God is acting, moving, and watching over His Word to perform it in my life. I trust that God is putting a period at the end of things. He's bringing situations in my life to a good conclusion in every area of my life, so I live in the zone of peace!

Queen, the appearance of things on the outside means nothing. When you live from Truth, your "real reality" is the life that you live from. It is where you make all adjustments that ultimately alter your present reality.

When you release the past and live from within—wholeheartedly with a sense of wonder, joy, and gratitude—there is a divine aligning that takes place. Things, people, and circumstances begin to fall into order, but that doesn't cause peace.

Your acceptance that peace is already in order within you creates the peace outside of you. Your outer doesn't dictate your inner. Your inner peace dictates your outer peace.

Decide from this moment to be at peace. Decide that nothing will steal your sense of joy. Be determined and diligent about looking for the treasure chest of good in the people around you and in all of the things that you experience. Rest in your imagination of good.

Let go of your old programs. Say goodbye to them once and for all. Say hello to peace. She's been waiting to be welcomed in. Make a home for Her in your heart, and mind and watch Her divine fruits in your life. Say hello to peace.

Hello peace!

Queen Reflections...

Queen, decide right now that anything that has compromised your peace must go! What are they? Make a decision that peace is the state that you live in and handle your business. Write what you are going to do differently.

Karin Haysbert

DAY THIRTY-SEVEN

Surrender:
Now That's Serenity

Peace Queen!

Letting go. Surrender. Sometimes, we want the "best "for others and we feel that it is our job to inform them of what we think is best for them and to make them do it, too. No. Our job is to work on us and love and release them. That includes our children. We don't always know what's best for them, but we think we do. What seems obvious to us may be counterproductive to their growth. Hmmm. We look at everything from our perspective.

It is difficult to see anything completely from another's point of view because we haven't lived in their minds and bodies, or walked in their shoes. We can ask God to help us to understand as best we can, but we must then trust God and the "God in them" to lead them to Life.

Letting go. Surrender. True serenity is indeed found in the surrender of the serenity prayer.

"Lord grant me the serenity to accept the things I cannot change, the courage to change the things I can, and the wisdom to know the difference."

Lord, give me total peace to let go, release, and surrender control of things. Help me to allow others to have their journey, to love and accept them anyway, and to truly let go and let God.

God, give me the courage, the strength, to look within, and make the changes and adjustments that I can make. Help me to face everything with the confidence of faith, taking full responsibility for my changes, and to act with boldness.

And then Lord, please give me divine wisdom and revelation to discern when to move forward and when to stand still, when to hold on and when to let go. Let me have total peace in spirit, soul, and body about it. Give me the peace that passes all understanding.

There's something so powerful about surrender.

When I surrender to the Truth of who I am and to who God is, it leads to serenity. When I surrender to the letting go of what's not my business to control, that's serenity.

When I surrender the fears and face them with faith, that's serenity.

Surrender Queen! Surrender and walk into your serenity.

Queen Reflections...

Queen, what do you have to surrender in order to live in your serenity? What courageous act must you take? Seek God's wisdom. What is He saying to you?

DAY THIRTY-EIGHT

Receive the Gifts

Peace Queen!

I was on the phone with my mom. She told me about an event that was giving away school supplies in the inner city that her friend's ministry was having. She wanted to see if the girls were available to go with her. They weren't, but even if they were, I told her that I felt uncomfortable with taking anything because

I'm not needy.

"I can buy my own school supplies, Mom. Besides, if I take them, that would mean that someone else who is needy can't have them." Right then, my mom said, "No! You have to be able to RECEIVE Karin. I used to be that way, too. It's not based on need. It's sowing and reaping. You are a giver, and you should receive." I paused and thought about it. Hmm. She was right.

What did receiving have to do with being needy?

Why did I feel that way? Was it pride? If I were in the line receiving school supplies, would I look like I was needy? Was that it? What if someone saw me who knew who I was? They might think, "What are YOU doing here?" Was I being selfish by taking it when I could easily buy them myself? Or was it much deeper than all of these?

The next day, I went to church, late, a little flustered because I had missed praise and worship and I needed to be in the Presence of the Lord through worship this morning especially. When my pastor took the stage, he said, "We're going to praise and worship God more this morning. God is saying that you NEED it!" THANK YOU! For the next 20 minutes, we entered into a powerful time of praise and thanksgiving that blessed my soul!

God heard me.

He heard my heart's cry, and the Spirit of God refilled me. Her sweet Presence let me know that all of the things that I was worrying about were settled. I RECEIVED it! God even went further. My pastor augmented his sermon and talked only about…

RECEIVING!

True story. He said that the God of miracles was in the house, and it was our day of RECEIVING! What was hard would now become easy, and there would be a flow that would come as we got into alignment with the Spirit of God. "Faithful" is all I could say.

Queen, in Luke 11:9-10, 13, the Word says, "Ask, and it will be given to you; seek, and you will find; knock, and it

will be opened to you. For everyone who asks RECEIVES...."
It goes further to say "... how much more will your heavenly
Father give the Holy Spirit to those who ASK Him!"

So what is the blockage in your receiving?

Having been born on a pew and raised in church all of
my life, I realize that there are still many things that I am
unlearning. I grew up hearing that there are none righteous,
that no one is worthy of God's goodness, and that we don't
deserve it. I understand what they were trying to do, but
those words wound the spirit of Man and instead of making
us humble, that is, not proud and arrogant, it humiliates and
makes us lose pride, respect, and dignity in the magnificence
of WHO we really are.

Beware of what humiliates you rather than humbles you.

It causes us to be works-based...I can only get, if I do. I
can only receive if I give. I realize the reality of sowing and
reaping, and I trust in the laws of the universe. However, there
are many things that God freely gives to us and we freely
receive—perhaps we just are not conscious of them. Truth is
that:

In order for us to GIVE, we first RECEIVE from God.

So I began to think...

I take breaths in and out. God freely gives it and I freely
receive. The sun shines without my doing a thing, and I
wholeheartedly receive the rays of her goodness. I am

worthy of receiving just because God made me and sent me here. And, the truth is, I AM an excellent receiver already.

So today, I make myself aware of the many ways that I already receive and attune my mind to open up and receive in all areas. I am worthy! It's simply God's divine love that makes me worthy and my alignment to it that empowers me to take in all of His blessings!

I receive the gifts!

Queen Reflections...

Wow! This is one of my biggest lessons, Queen. So what did you see about receiving that you hadn't seen before? What are some of your blockages to receiving? Make a commitment to identify the areas where you are receiving and open your mind and heart to receive more. Write it out.

For more on this chapter, go to www.queenarise.com.

Karin Haysbert

DAY THIRTY-NINE

Emptying Your Bucket

Peace Queen!

What's on your bucket list? Today, we had the honor of fulfilling one of our mom's bucket list desires of riding a horse. As she put it, riding "a real live horse" (laughing out loud). It was so gratifying to see the wonder in her eyes as that wish was fulfilled in our "Dare to Thrive at 75" birthday celebration of Mom. We have spent an entire week on a cruise with my parents celebrating Mom and showing our love and appreciation for her.

Each day, we planned activities and events that would be not just fun but would also stretch her too, like parasailing. We even have video footage of parasailing Granny! We took Mom to an "Uptown Funk" dance class. Yes, Pastor Dee was funking it up on stage in a choreographed dance. She was hesitant at first, but by the end of the class, during the Soul Train Line, she was spinning so freely that her birthday crown flew off of her head! We also incorporated things that were simply "wishes" for her.

The Make-A-Wish Foundation is loved for that very reason. It makes the wishes of others come true. So, how about you? This is two-fold.

What are your wishes?

Again, what's on your bucket list? Do you even know? So many of us do not. I talk to women all over this world. We spend so much time catering to the needs and desires of others and forget about ourselves. Neither God nor anyone else can help make an unidentified desire come to pass.

Yes, God knows what we have need of, and He knows what we desire before we ask. Yet, He still wants us to ask. In order to ask, you must know. What do you want? Let's explore this.

What do you love? What do you desire? What would give you great joy? What would make you feel so good inside? Can you start seeing yourself with it? Can you imagine yourself doing it? If you can, it's coming! Write it all down. Things that are written down have a higher probability of being fulfilled.

Give life to your wishes by writing them down.

Today, why don't you grant a wish? How can you, no matter how large or small it is, make another's wish or desire come true? There is such joy and fulfillment in giving. It will bless you as much as or even more than it blesses the recipient. Make the person's wish come true. And, know that someone else is on the way to do the same for you. So Queen, get to writing. Start filling up your bucket list so it can start being emptied out into your life.

Queen Reflections...

Take some time right now and think about what you really want. Ponder about what would give you life! Start making that list. And, add to this list regularly. Give thanks and celebrate wishes fulfilled. And, search for whom you can bless today.

Karin Haysbert

DAY FORTY

A Nouveau Feminist?

Peace Queen!

Feminism. It is a word that until recently made me sort of cringe within. It evoked images of angry women burning bras who were vociferous in their hatred towards men. Even though I can understand anger about any injustice, I know that...

Anger cannot be the fuel used to solve the problems coming from injustice.

Dr. Martin Luther King, Jr. and many others taught us that. Anger may cause you to stand up, but like all fear-based emotions, it can lead you astray so that you begin to fight for the sake of fighting. Anger—or more precisely, fear—can cause your vision to be altered so that you fight the wrong "enemy" and many times end up fighting, biting, and devouring yourselves. That is what I believe happened in old feminism. We, as women, began to turn against one another and limited our progress.

The nouveau feminism, in my opinion, is based on

188

truth—the truth that we all are worthy, deserving, divine beings. We are equal in our value regardless of gender or any other designation.

Truth is, we are all spirit. We all came from the nostrils of God, every single one of us. We all have divine birthrights, and none of them include any higher status based on gender.

I know that some teach that God made Adam and then He made Eve. We've been told or made to believe that Eve was sort of an afterthought and that she was sent to just help Adam. In some ways, I think people have taken that to mean that man is more important or valuable than woman. Really? How so?

We all existed at the same time because we are all spirit and came from God. Scriptures only tell of God simply forming Eve's body after forming Adam's but Eve always was, just like each of us always were. Additionally, the Word that says God made "man" is translated mankind, of which male and females are a part of. Adam was "pregnant" (for lack of a better term) with Eve and all of the rest of mankind. That's why God put him to sleep to pull us OUT of him. Just my thoughts…

We all eternally existed in God. God simply appointed moments for each of us to appear in time here. I am no more valuable than my children because I came into time sooner. Selah! (Which means pause and think about that!)

So the nouveau feminism, I think, values women, all women, for our strengths and our wonderful differences from not just men but also from we each other, too. It highlights our God-given power and says that we will not think less of ourselves and will not allow anyone to put us into boxes of any form, male or female. I believe it is truly about self-love, self-acceptance, and authenticity.

Loving me does not mean that I do not or cannot love you, too. It simply means that I love, honor, respect, and accept myself. That really is the first step to loving anyone else. Loving myself means that I will teach others how to treat me by how I treat myself.

To me, the nouveau feminism can be a unifying movement that recognizes that every woman's path is different and that's OK. Maybe this isn't new at all. Maybe it's just new to me in its terminology, but I love it. I live it. I'm learning it. And, it's what I teach already.

While I realize that the word feminism may still have a buzz for others, that wouldn't be unlike the many who have that same feeling when Christianity or any other religion is mentioned. Truth is, millions have been killed and maimed physically, mentally, emotionally, and spiritually in the name of our religions. Yet, that doesn't stop me from what I know to be true about my beliefs.

With that said, I stand for the truth in this new feminism. I guess I am a nouveau feminist. Yes I am!

Queen Reflections…

So how about you? What comes up for you when you hear the term feminism? While I don't think I'll be marching about it anywhere, I certainly live it. I believe that religion, culture, and our own self-oppression have done a number on women in keeping us down and bound. Learning to love and value ourselves and to see ourselves through God's eyes are key. What are your thoughts?

Karin Haysbert

BONUS 1

Losing My Religion

Peace Queen!

It's a song that I remember the refrain from years ago. And today, it's the melody of my heart. Religion.

Religion to me is man's attempt to control a spiritual relationship through natural means.

Religion hasn't always been detrimental to me, but just like rat poison is mostly good cornhusks, it's the little bit of poison that makes it deadly. For me, religion's traps pushed me away from truth—the truth about God, the truth about myself, and the truth about others. Overall, the truth about the universe and how it works.

The bondage of religion pressed me down. It made me feel less than, unworthy, and undeserving. It made me afraid to read anything except the Bible. It separated me from anyone who wasn't "saved."

Religion called everything that was unfamiliar "the devil" and demonic, and it made it something to be feared. As we know, fear is the basis of all the evil in the hearts of men and in our world.

Religion made me judgmental, deciding people's fates and sending people to hell. Religion caused me to say that ONLY "we" are right. You're just deceived. Religion puts God, the Unlimited Source of Life and Light, into a box that I could figure out and that we can turn pages to explain Him. Religion made me a "know-it-all," prideful, and pharisaical. But then I met her. I met a woman when I was hurt, disappointed, and crying out to God for answers.

I had done everything I was told by church folks to do. I read. I studied. I fasted. I prayed. I was confessing but still not possessing. I'd done everything, I thought, to serve, to be excellent, to give to others, to self-sacrifice, and to crucify myself. All I got were nail prints in my hands and feet, a pierced side, and a crown of thorns on my head. I had misery but no victory.

I felt victimized, disregarded, and unappreciated. In my mind, it was all "their fault." The "devil" was busy. Maybe, I needed to fast and pray more. Perhaps, I didn't have the right scriptures. Oh I know. I needed to sow a seed for the breakthrough and on and on.

But when I met her, my eyes began to open. Who is she? Louise Hay. What? Don't let religion stop you. This woman's work did more to free me than I can even say. As I read her words, I realized something that I hadn't heard often, if ever, in church. I'm not just loved. I'd heard that. As I read her work I realized:

I am lovable. I am deserving. I am acceptable. And, I am worthy just because I'm here.

I also began to realize on a much deeper level that all that was happening around me was merely a reflection of what was going on within me. In most cases, it was NOT the devil. It wasn't my mother, my father, my husband, my ex, or my children.

It was ME.

It was my own thinking and the beliefs that I was unacceptable, unlovable, unworthy, and undeserving that had led me to that point of despair.

As I delved deeper, I began to take responsibility for my life. I began to be accountable for my own points of attraction. I started to see myself as the wonderful, divine creation that God sees me as. I started to let go of the religious dogma that kept me oppressed, controlled, and unconscious of the beauty of my being. I got more serious about hearing God's voice for myself than I ever had. I began to approve of me so I didn't need others' approval as much.

Slowly, gradually, I began to drift away from the shore of my own familiarity and into the ocean of the unknown. It was so scary. It still is sometimes. My feet didn't touch the bottom here, but I felt upheld. I was upheld by love. For once in my life, I began to FEEL really loved, appreciated, honored, respected, and accepted. I did because I gave those things to myself.

They were always there. God's love for me contained all that I needed and much, much more, but until I opened my heart to receive it, it was like a trove of treasure hidden within an unguarded cave waiting for my discovery.

For me, it started with taking an honest assessment of my life. It began with being open to seeing what I really believed and WHY. As I truthfully evaluated my life and asked myself, "How's that working for you, Karin?" I began to see that many of my religious attitudes destroyed my own self-esteem, sabotaged my relationships, and made life that was meant to be "life to the full until it overflows" into one of day-to-day misery. Reading, thinking, asking questions, and waiting for answers set me FREE and continues to free me more daily.

Silence became my best friend.

In religion, I had to pray a certain way. I felt compelled to say these scriptures and to follow this mold in order to get to God.

In relationship, I can sit quietly and commune with God in my heart and that's enough. "Help" is a prayer and it's no less powerful than a whole night of crying out.

In religion, I had to fight the devil, put on war clothes, wail, and cry.

In relationship, I can look honestly at the thought patterns that I'm thinking that's opening the door to fear. I can press into the love of God and simply release fear. My biggest fight is with ME. I know that what I resist persists. I had already believed that so many people use the devil as an excuse not to deal with themselves, but now, I know it to be true.

In religion, if I had not prayed for a certain amount of time, I felt uncovered.

In relationship, I pray without ceasing. I'm checking in all throughout the day. I realize that my very thoughts, the words I say, the things I do ARE prayers. So now I can guard my heart, my ways, and how I FEEL more diligently.

In religion, feelings were discounted. I was told "not to be moved by how I feel."

In relationship, I now know that feelings are so very important. We live in a feeling universe. This whole world is energy. So my feelings, emotions—the energy produced within me as a result of my thoughts—are of utmost importance. They indicate where I'm really going.

Thoughts and words are the car, but feelings are the fuel.

I won't go anywhere with all my confessions and all of my prayers until I FEEL it. Until I really believe it within. Until I can sense it within. See it, smell it, hear it, taste it, and touch it—all those words can turn into just vain babblings, so I FEEL my way to faith's manifestation.

Religion told me that I need someone, some church leader, something out there to approve of me and to give me permission to BE and to DO what I was made to do. Religion said that God was way up there somewhere, separated from me.

Relationship tells me that God is in me. God who is expressing Himself as me is never separated from me. My Father and I are ONE. And further, the Father's approval is all that I need and actually has already been given to me. I am accepted as God's beloved now.

196

I could go on and on, but suffice it to say that losing my religion has given me LIFE, imparted the freedom to be the magnificent me that I was created to be and has unleashed parts of me that I didn't know existed. It has transformed my perspective on life, opened my heart, and made me more compassionate and far less judgmental. It's allowed me to release control and yet take responsibility for my life in empowering ways.

Losing my religion has given me the wisdom to not enforce my will on anyone else's. It has allowed me to let others have their journeys. Losing my religion has opened my eyes to the GOOD in myself and in others. It has given me the hope to expect good everywhere that I go.

Losing my religion has strengthened me to see God, as He is, a God of love. I know that God is not mad at me, looking to find me doing something "wrong" in order to punish me. Losing my religion has allowed me to let go of the ways that I punish others and myself. It's allowed me to release the guilt and shame that I had permitted to hold me captive.

In letting the past be passed, I now see all circumstances as good. I can now truly "give thanks in all things." I learn the lessons and release the pain. Losing my religion set me free from what I call the "submission omissions." I now know who I am as a woman, standing in my feminine power, and I am no longer held down by the fear-written laws of male dominance or control.

With that said, losing my religion has helped me to wipe the slate of my heart clean of the pain in my relationships with men. So now, I can look at them with love and acceptance and seek to first understand them more than to be understood by them. I can see them as the Kings that they are and honor and respect them as such.

Losing my religion has set me FREE.

Free on this level. I know that there's much more to let go of and to go into, but what I can say is this: It's been the journey of my lifetime and it FEELS really, really good, losing my religion!

Queen Reflections…

How can losing your religion lead you to greater life? Lean further into the Truth Queen. God is not into religion. He is into relationship. If you study history, you will see that most world religions have a political agenda. It's an agenda to control the masses. Read your Bible. Study history. Jesus was constantly at odds with the religious, political parties: the Pharisees and the Sadducees. He did not come to set up a new religion. He came to lead us to LIFE, to relationship, and to the Father's love!

So what religious garb do you need to shed to be naked and unashamed before God? Religion is our sewing of fig leaves in part to cover ourselves because we feel shame and guilt about what we've done or the lies that we believe about who we are. God wants relationship, not religion. I encourage you to revisit this again and again and to keep writing what comes up for you.

For more on this chapter, go to www.queenarise.com.

Karin Haysbert

BONUS 2

I Have a Dream, Too!

Peace Queen!

Today is the day that we celebrate the "Man and the Dream," Dr. Martin Luther King, Jr. This dream was one that has forever changed the course of history. It was not just a dream that people of all races, cultures, genders, and beliefs were able to live next door to each other, holding hands, swaying, singing, "Kumbaya."

It was a dream of a better NOW for all people based on love and acceptance with economic empowerment at the heart of it. Yes. Get your paper Queen!

There are no civil rights without silver rights.

There is no empowerment without economic empowerment...not in this society! It's called the Golden Rule. She who holds the gold makes the rules. I'll come back to that.

So, let's get clear about being financially free. I define financial freedom as being able to make decisions for my life without being hindered in any way because of finances. That varies from person to person based on your purpose.

Financial freedom gives us the ability to be a blessing without hesitation.

We should be able to help others without thoughts of fear of not having enough for others and ourselves. Our giving should be accompanied by peace. Financial freedom empowers us to never be bought and sold. We can give and serve more from a place of strength and clarity.

So, I have a dream, too! I have a dream for Queens to be FREE.

FREE to be able to stand in our Truth.
FREE to fully articulate our genius.
FREE to make our own choices based on faith and not fear.
FREE to give love and to receive the love.
FREE to live our inner wealth so that our outer wealth is fully expressed.

I have a dream of Queens living 3 John 2.

I have a dream that we prosper and are in health because our souls prosper. I have a dream. I have a dream of Queens reigning with our Kings. I dream of Kings and Queens ruling in love and harmony. I dream of royal families in which children know their divine destiny and confidently live it. I have a dream, too.

As with all world-changing dreams, the dream begins with me and the dream begins with you. So daily, I work to let the Queen arise in me so that I am able to lead the way for others. I rule from the gold, the wealth that is within me. Will you join me?

Here I am Lord. Send me. I Have a dream!

Queen Reflections...

Well, Queen, we are at the end of your journey, but it's really just the beginning. YOU are a different woman now. You have grown and stretched, and now you are closer to your dreams than you were before because you have BECOME more! What is your dream? Has it shifted since you began this journey? Write about it.

_____

_____

_____

_____

_____

_____

_____

_____

_____

_____

_____

_____

_____

_____

_____

_____

_____

_____

Karin Haysbert

THANK YOU!!!

Peace Queen!

I'm honored that you have allowed me into your heart and home, and that you have made it to the end of my first book. (Hint. Stay tuned for other works coming soon!) Do you want more? Does your soul cry for an even deeper dive into you to allow the Queen within to arise? I hope so.

This has been part of my journey and the process that God took me through to a closer, more authentic relationship with Him. The adventure continues. So where are you in yours? Have these writings inspired you to go even deeper? Do you need someone to walk this walk with you?

If you have felt a soul connection with me, let's talk about it. I have a number of classes on my website that will minister to you and take you from where you are to where you desire to be. Additionally, I offer programs to help to liberate the Queen within you and to set you on the course to fulfill your divine destiny. I am an expert at taking spiritual truths and weaving them into practical strategies to empower Queens worldwide to confidently stand in the fullness of who they are to live their dreams. I can help you to fulfill your passionate purpose in the earth. Here's how to connect with me.

Website: www.queensforchrist.org
E-mail: support@queensforchrist.org
Facebook, YouTube, and Instagram: @thequeensforchrist
Twitter and Periscope: @queensforchrist

Hope to talk with you soon. Stay tuned for my upcoming books… I have many on the way! Until we meet again, keep on reigning with the King. Queen arise!

Much Love,

Queen Karin

63192920R00115

Made in the USA
Charleston, SC
30 October 2016